THE LIFE OF THE MAHĀSIDDHA TILOPA

by

Mar-pa Chos-kyi bLo-gros

Translated by
Fabrizio Torricelli and
Āchārya Sangye T. Naga

Edited by
Vyvyan Cayley

LIBRARY OF TIBETAN WORKS AND ARCHIVES

First Edition 1995
Second Edition 2003
Third Edition 2011

ISBN: 81-85102-91-0

Published by the Library of Tibetan Works and Archives, Dharamsala, H.P. and printed at Indraprastha Press (CBT), 4 Bahadurshah Zafar Marg, New Delhi-110002.

Contents

Foreword

We are pleased to publish this short work on the life of the Indian mahāsiddha Tilopa, which appears to have been composed in the 11th century by the great Marpa Lotsawa Chos-kyi bLo-gros of Tibet.

This text is an account of the 'complete liberation' of the guru of Naropa; as such it will be appreciated not only by disciples of the Kagyud-pa tradition of Tibetan Buddhism, but also by others interested in the lives of the Buddhist saints and masters.

The work has been ably and devotedly translated by Italian scholar Fabrizio Torricelli in collaboration with Sangye Tendar Naga from our own Research and Translation Bureau. We delight in the merit they gain by making this text accessible to the reading public. In addition to the translation, they have provided a transliteration of the original Tibetan script for scholars who wish to read the account in both languages.

May the contents of this book be beneficial for all beings and help to spread the rays of Buddhism throughout the world.

Gyatsho Tshering
Director

January 1995

Preface

The text we present is the earliest biography of the *mahāsiddha* Tilopa of which we have direct knowledge. In fact, from the dedicatory verses and the colophon, it appears to have been composed by the great dKar-brgyud-pa master Mar-pa Chos-kyi-blo-gros (1012-1097) for the benefit of his son Dar-ma mDo-sde.[1]

It is a short work included in a collection of texts of the Mar-pa dKar-brgyud-pa tradition: *bDe-mchog mkha'-'gro snyan-rgyud,* vol. *kha—brGyud-pa yid-bzhin-nor-bu'i rnam-par thar-pa,* fols. 1b-11b. Such texts are connected with the oral tradition (*snyan-rgyud*) transmitted by the disciple of Mi-la-ras-pa, Ras-chung rDo-rje-grags (1084-1161) and, because of that, they are known as *Ras-chung snyan-rgyud.* The manuscript, compiled by Shar-kha Ras-chen, Kun-dga'-dar-po and Byang-chub-bzang-po in the first half of the 16th century, is written in a cursive script (*dbu-med*), which is known as *khams-bris,* where many short forms are attested.

As to the genre, it belongs to what we could call "Buddhist hagiology", being an account of the 'complete liberation' (Tib. *rnam-par thar-pa,* Skt. *vimokṣa*) of the *guru* of Nāropa. These *rnam-thar,* G. Tucci (1949: 150-151) has written,

> ... must be considered neither histories nor chronicles. The events they relate with a particular satisfaction are spiritual conquests, visions and ecstasies; they follow the long apprenticeship through which man becomes divine, they give lists of the texts upon which saints trained and

disciplined their minds, for each lama they record the masters who opened up his spirit to serene visions, or caused the ambrosia of supreme revelations to rain down upon him. Human events have nothing to do with these works, [...]. Kings, princes and the great ones of this world have no place there, or they only appear as helpful and pious patrons. Every happening is thus seen in the light of spiritual triumphs.

A contextual reading of other *Ti-lo-pa'i rnam-thar* which are available has been necessary in order to understand some difficult expressions and puzzling passages in our text: especially because of the so often wrong, or unusual, spelling of many words. The most useful hagiographic sources[2] we sifted through are the following:

—rGyal-thang-pa bDe-chen-rdo-rje (13th cent.), *rJe-btsun chen-po Tilli-pa'i rnam-par thar-pa*, in *dKar-brgyud gser-'phreng*, fols. 1a-22a. The English 'Preface' to the reproduction of the manuscript has the following observation to make on rGyal-thang-pa: "No biography of this master is immediately available, but it is known that he was a disciple of rGod-tshang-pa mGon-po-rdo-rje (1189-1258), the last guru whose biography appears in this collection." The manuscript, following the 'Brug-pa dKar-brgyud-pa tradition, can be dated to the latter half of the 15th century or the first half of the 16th century and it is preserved at Hemis in Ladakh.

—Grub-thob O-rgyan-pa Rin-chen-dpal (1229/30-1309), *Te-lo-pa'i rnam-thar*, in *bKa'-brgyud yid-bzhin-nor-bu-yi 'phreng-ba*, fols. 7a-26a. Like rGyal-thang-pa, O-rgyan-pa was a disciple of rGod-tshang-pa. However, he integrated the teachings of this master with the instruction he received from a ḍākinī in Uḍḍiyāṇā (Tucci 1940; Tucci 1949: 90-91). This collection of hagiographies, following the 'Bri-gung dKar-brgyud-pa tradition, was written between 1295 and 1304 and is conserved in the library of the Kangyur Rimpoche of Darjeeling.

—rDo-rje-mdzes-'od (13th cent.), *rJe-Te-lo-pa'i rnam-thar,* in *bKa'-brgyud-kyi rnam-thar chen-mo rin-po-che'i gter-mdzod dgos-'dod 'byung-gnas,* fols. 27a-43b. The author was a disciple of dPal-ldan Ri-khrod-dbang-phyug, who was a disciple of 'Jig-rten mGon-po, the founder of the 'Bri-gung-pa sect. This text has been of particular use during our work because it is the only one which has been translated into English so far (*Great Kagyu Masters*: 33-54).

—Mon-rtse-pa Kun-dga'-dpal-ldan (1408-1475?), *Ti-lo Shes-rab-bzang-po'i rnam-par thar-pa,* in *dKar-brgyud gser-'phreng,* vol. *kha,* fols. 12a-23b. The manuscript, compiled and calligraphed in the last half of the 15th century and conserved at Takna in Ladakh, brings together a collection of hagiographies following the 'Ba'-ra 'Brug-pa dKar-brgyud-pa tradition.

—gTsang-smyon He-ru-ka Sangs-rgyas-rgyal-mtshan (1452-1507), *Ti-lo-pa'i rnam-thar,* in *bDe-mchog mkha'-'gro snyan-rgyud,* vol. *ga,* fols. 9b-20a. This biography of Tilopa is included in a *Ras-chung snyan-rgyud* which was compiled at the end of the 15th century. Even if the dating of the manuscript is quite difficult to achieve, "stylistically, a dating to the second half of the 16th century is not unreasonable."[3] This manuscript (Ms. A) is known as the Bya-btang 'Phrin-las-dpal-'bar Manuscript; there is another set of the same *bDe-mchog mkha'-'gro snyan-rgyud*

(Ms. B), known as the Gra-dkar Rab-'jam-pa Manuscript, but references here are given only from the former.

—'Bri-gung Chos-rje Kun-dga'-rin-chen (1475-1527), *rJe-btsun Ti-lo-pa'i rnam-thar dbang-bzhi'i chu-rgyun,* in *bKa'-rgyud bla-ma-rnams-kyi rnam-thar rin-chen gser-'phreng,* fols. 11b-13b (fol. 12 is missing). This concise text was composed in 1508 by the last abbot of 'Bri-gung monastery to follow the pure 'Bri-gung bKa'-brgyud-pa tradition. In fact, after him the rNying-ma-pa school gradually took over the monastery.

—dBang-phyug-rgyal-mtshan (16th cent.), *rJe-btsun Ti-lo'i rnam-par thar-pa,* in *bKa'-brgyud gser-'phreng rgyas-pa,* fols. 1a-45a. This manuscript, preserved in the monastery of rDzong-khul in Zangskar, is the only one (Ms. A) from which we give references. There is however another manuscript, *rJe-btsun Ti-lo-pa dang Nā-ro-pa'i rnam-thar rin-po-che* (Ms. B fols. 1b-68a), which is a part of the same collection of hagiographies following the 'Brug-pa dKar-brgyud-pa tradition. The author, who was a disciple of gTsang-smyon He-ru-ka, wrote this *rnam-thar* in 1523 at rDza-ri bSam-gtan Gling.

—lHa-btsun Rin-chen-rnam-rgyal (1473-1557), *Sangs-rgyas thams-cad-kyi rnam-'phrul rje-btsun Ti-lo-pa'i rnam-mgur,* fols. 1a-38a. One of the closest disciples of gTsang-smyon He-ru-ka, lHa-btsun faithfully follows the teachings and contents of the oral tradition going back to Ras-chung. This text is particularly beautiful and interesting because it is the only *rnam-mgur* of Tilopa's we have, i.e. a *rnam-thar* interspersed with esoteric songs (*mgur*). These songs are by Tilopa himself and belong to two texts which are in the tantric section (*rgyud-'grel*) of the *bsTan-'gyur,* the *Acintyamahāmudrā*[4] and the *Mahāmudropadeśa.*[5]

lHa-bstun compiled this *rnam-mgur* and printed it first in 1550 at Brag-dkar-rta-so. Even if there is another available source of the same text (Ms. B fols. 1a-24a), our references are only from the former (Ms. A).

After the edition of the text, the Tibetan original of the poetical passages has been given together with its English version, in order to assist the reader's comprehension of our attempt at translation.

Fabrizio Torricelli and Sangye T. Naga

Transliteration of the Tibetan Text

[1b.1]	folio and line number
[*xx*]	emendation of what precedes
(xx)	uncertain text
[[xx]]	to be deleted

—0—

[1b.1] // Na mo gu ru de ba ḍā ki ni / sa ma yā ma nu sma ra / si dhyaṃ tu ye /
spros bral mkha' khyab gar dgu'i nyams kyi gdul bya smin byed [1b.2] sku gsum las / mtsho chen mi g.yam [*mi-g.yo*] cung zad dangs (dvangs) pa'i sku gsum mkha' 'gro'i rba rlabs can // chu skyes bde chen 'bras bu dngos sprul 'gro mgon shes rab bzang po [1b.3] dang / bcu gnyis bar du dka' ba rab spyad nā ro'i paṇ chen de la 'dud /

/ gang zhig sku gsum nor bu la /
/ gang gis mi shes rgyas gdab[1] pa /
/ mkha' 'gro'i gsang tshig [2a.1] lde mig gi /
/ rnam gsum nor bu rab tu stan bya'o [*bstan-bya'o*] /

/ ngo sprod yid bzhin nor bu yis /
/ chos kyi sku la nga sprod [*ngo-sprod*] bya /
/ rmi lam yid bzhin nor [2a.2] bu yis /
/ longs sku lus la bzhug par bya /
/ brgyud pa yid bzhin nor bu yis /
/ chos sku dngos su stan par bya'o /[2]

/ mkha' 'gro'i snyan brgyud nyi ma'i 'od gsal la /
/ lha min sgra khcan [*sgra-gcan*[3]] [2a.3] brjod pas rab 'jigs nas /

/ mdo sde'i don phyir[4] yi ger bkod pa la /
/ mkha' 'gros bzod gsol byin gyis rlobs /

/ snyan brgyud gdam pa [*gdams-pa*] kun la stan pa min /
/ [2a.4] ltogs kyang pha ma'i sha la bza' ba min /
/ khye [*khe*] 'ang tsan dug [*btsan-dug*] sbyar ba 'tshong pa min /
/ gtad mo [*ltad-mo*] che'ang rang gi snying sprul ston pa min //

de la mkha' 'gro ma'i snyan brgyud [2b.1] ngo mtshar can la gsum te [*ste*] / ston byed slob dpon gyi mtshan nyid dang / stan pa [*bstan-pa*] slob ma'i mtshan nyid dang / stan bya [*bstan-bya*] chos kyi gnas lugs so // dang po ni / nyams rtogs brgyud pa thugs rje dang ldan pa la [2b.2] sogs pa'o // gnyis pa ni / rang gi brgyud la tshe gcig lus gcig la sangs rgyas 'tshol nus pa la sogs pa'o // gsum pa stan bya [*bstan-bya*] chos kyi gnas lugs la gsum te [*ste*] / phyi sgro 'dogs spyod byed sprul pa sku'i gdam pa [*gdams-pa*] / [2b.3] brgyud pa yid bzhin nor bu dang / nang nyams len longs spyod rdzogs pa sku'i gdam pa [*gdams-pa*] smin lam yid bzhin nor bu dang / gsang pa ngo sprod chos sku'i gdam pa [*gdams-pa*] grol lam yid bzhin nor bu'o //
de las 'di sprul pa sku'i [2b.4] gdams pa brgyud pa yid bzhin nor bu yin no // de la chos sku ye shes mkha' 'gro ma'i lo rgyus dang / sprul sku grub thob brgyud pa'i lo rgyus gnyis las / dang po ni / sangs rgyas thams cad sku gsum du bzhugs pa ltar ye shes kyi [3a.1] mkha' 'gro ma 'di'ang sku gsum du bzhugs te rgyas par 'og tu 'chad par 'gyur ro // gnyis pa sprul sku grub thob brgyud pa'i rnam thar la thog mar te lo'i rnam thar la bzhi ste / dang po mi rang rgyud [3a.2] par grags pa dang / bde mchog gi sprul par grags pa dang / bde mchog dngos su grags pa dang / sangs rgyas thams cad kyi sku 'dus par grags pa'o //

—1—

De las dang po jo bo chen po te lo pa 'di mi rang rgyud par byas na sku che ba'i yon tan la bzhi ste / [3a.3] dang po drang don du mkha' 'gros lung bstan te bla ma rtsal te [*btsal-te*] sgrub pa mdzad pa dang / mkha' 'gro zil gyis mnan te chos zhus pa dang / nges don du mi'i bla ma med par[5] stan pa [*bstan-pa*] dang / sprul pa sna tshogs stan pa'o [*bstan-pa'o*] //

—1.1—

De las dang po [3a.4] te lo pa ni / rgya gar shar phyogs za hor gyi yul grong khyer dza ko zhes bya ba na / yab bram ze gsal ba / yum bram ze gsal ldan ma / sring mo bram ze gsal ba'i sgron ma gsum yod pa las // sras med par gyur te phyi [3a.5] nang gi rten thams cad la mchod pa phul nas gsol ba btab pas sras gcig btsas par gyur te / de'i tshe rgya gar shar phyogs thams cad 'od kyis khyab par byung pas mtshan gsal 'od du btags / de nas bram ze mtshan mkhan la [3b.1] bris (dris) pas / des smras pa

/ 'di ni lha klu gnod sbyin nam /
/ sangs rgyas gang yin ma 'tshal bas /
/ skyes bu mchog 'di gces par skyongs /

/ zhes zer ba bzhin / de gces par skyong ba'i dus re zhig na yab phyir thal [3b.2] nas yum sras gnyis yod pa dang / hrib ma hrib pa gcig byung nas bltas pas bud med mi sdug pa'i mtshan ma can / kha phus 'debs pa 'theng zhing mkhar ba la rten pa [*brten-pa*] mang po'i snang pa [*snang-ba*] byung nas / ma'i bsam pa [3b.3] la 'dre yin nam / bu 'di rang 'chi'am snyam pa las / bud med rnams kyis smras pa

/ gces par skyangs [*bskyangs*] kyang mi 'chi ba'i /
/ sa phyogs dag kyang yod ma yin /

/ ces (zhes) zer ro // mas 'o na thabs ci byas na phan ces (zhes) [3b.4] gris pas [*dris-pas*] / yang smras pa

/ bu ma he skyong zhing yi ge brlobs [*slobs*] /
/ mkha' 'gro ma yi lung bstan 'byung /

/ gsung nas gar song cha ṁed du thal skad //
de nas cher skyes pa dang de ltar byed du bcug pas / [3b.5] yang ma he skyong par sngar gyi bud med de byung nas / khyod kyi yul dang pha ma la sogs pa 'drir byung pa [*byung-ba*] la khye'u des smras pa /

/ yul ni shar phyogs dza ko.yin /
/ pha ni bram ze gsal ba yin /
/ ma ni bram ze gsal [4a.1] ldan yin /
/ sring mo bram ze gsal sgron yin /
/ nga rang bram ze gsal 'od yin /
/ shing 'di sha ba'i sdong po yin /
/ yi ge rlabs nas [*bslabs-nas*] dam chos byed /
/ ma he nor phyir skyong pa yin /

/ ces (zhes) byas pas / [4a.2] bud med de rnams khros pa'i tshul gyis bu khyed kyis mi shes par 'dug

/ yul ni nub phyogs u rgyan yin /
/ yab ni bde mchog 'khor lo yin /
/ yum ni rdo rje phag mo yin /
/ sring mo mkha' 'gro bde ster ma /
/ khyod rang paṇ tsa pa na yin /
/ [4a.3] dud 'gro ma he ma skyong por (bar) /
/ byang chub shing gi nags khrod du /
/ nyams myong ma he rgyun du skyongs /

/ zhes zer ro // der khye'us smras pa / de ngas skyong mi shes byas pas / sa la bhe ra ha'i [*bhe-ha-ra'i*] dur khrod du song shig (zhig) bla mas ston par 'gyur ro // [4a.4] zhes lung stan no [*lung-bstan-no*] //

de yang lho phyogs kyi rgyud nas sa la bhe ha ra[6] zhes bya ba dbang phyug chen pos byin gyis rlabs pa'i dur khrod yod de / der phyi nang gi mkha' 'gro ma rnams kyi tshogs kyi 'khor lo bskor ba'i tshe bram ze'i khye'us byon te / tsarya ba [*tsarya-pa*] [4a.5] la gdam pa [*gdams-pa*] 'ang zhus /

slob dpon chen po la wa pas

/ grong khyer chen po'i srang mdo[7] ru /
/ bcu gnyis bar du gnyid log pas / .
/ phyag rgya chen po'i dngos grub thob /

/ ces pas 'od gsal zhus /

klu sgrub btsal bas dur khrod de na brtul zhugs spyod pa'i [4a.6] rnal 'byor pa ma tang gi spyil po gcig na sgom gyin 'dug te / klu sgrub dri za'i rgyal po la chos bshod du song / skyes bu khyed rjes su 'dzin pa la nga btang pa yin gsung (gsungs) / der maṇḍala phul te zhus pas / dpal gsang ba 'dus pa'i [4a.7] dkyil 'khor dngos su sprul nas dbang bskur / brgyud [*rgyud*] bshad pas sems kyi ngo bo mthong /

der lha khang cig na zhang po'i brgyad stong pa [*brgya-stong-pa*] cig sgrog sar / bud med gcig byung nas 'di'i don shes sam zer / ma shes byas pas 'o na ngas bshad kyi zer nas [4b.1] de'i don bshad / he badzra dang / 'khor lo sdom pa'i dbang bskur dang rgyud bshad / lu hi pa'i dgongs pa 'di ltar yin pas bsgoms [*sgoms*] shig zer / zhang pos sgom du mi ster byas pas / brgya stong pa thag pa chod la lha khang gi kha nas chu la dor la / [4b.2] smyo rdzu thob la sgoms shig / ngas byin gyis rlabs pas brgya (brgyad) stong pa ci yang mi nyes zer nas de

ltar byas pas / brgya (brgyad) stong pa ci yang ma nyes[8] / smyo 'dug zer nas lcags bcug / de bde bar gshegs pa'i thugs gnyis su med pa la gsal bar snang ba'i lam thams cad kyi [4b.3] snying pa [*snying-po*] rim pa gnyis la gom (goms) par byas so //
de nas lung bstan pa

/ shar phyogs bhang ga la'i[9] brgyud /
/ paṇ tsha pa na'i tshong 'dus na /
/ smad 'tshong bha ri 'khor bcas kyi /
/ de'i [*de-yi*] zhabs 'breng byas na gsangs [*bsang*] /
/ spyod mthar thon nas dngos grub thob /

[4b.4] ces pa dang der phyin nas / mtshan bzhin skyes pa 'gugs pa dang skyel ba'i las byas // nyin bzhin til 'bru ba'i las byas pas rgya gar skad du[10] ti lo pa / bod skad du / til bsrungs zhabs zhes grags so //
de nas dur khrod ke re li zhes bya bar [4b.5] phyin nas bha ri ma gnyis gsang ba sngags kyi spyod pas[11] mnyes te / mthar phyin par mdzad do //
de nas yang tshong 'dus der til 'bru 'phro la phyag rgya chen po mchog la nye ba'i dngos grub thob par gyur to //
der grong khyer gyi mi rnams mthong [4b.6] tshul tha dad de 'ga' zhig gis ni me dpung 'bar [*pa*] bar mthong / 'ga' zhig gis rus rgyan la me 'bar bar mthong ste / mi rnams kyis gdam pa [*gdams-pa*] zhus pas / nga'i yid la skyes pa'i gnyug ma des brjes 'jug [*rjes-'jug*] khyed kyi snying la zhugs par byos [4b.7] shig / ces brjod pa dang / de ma thag tu grol bar gyur to //
de nas yul de'i rgyal po 'khor bcas glang po che la zhon nas snyen bskur (bsnyen bkur) la yongs (yong) pas / bram ze'i khye'u dang / bha ri ma gnyis kyis tshangs pa'i sgra chen pos rdo rje'i mgur bzhes pa/

/ [5a.1] gang zhig snying por zhugs pa til gyi mar /
/ rmongs pas til la yod par shes gyur kyang /
/ rten cing 'brel 'byung yan lag ma shes na /
/ til mar snying po 'byung par (bar) mi nus ltar /
/ lhan cig skyes pa [5a.2] gnyug ma'i ye shes de /
/ 'gro ba kun gyi snying la yod gyur kyang /
/ bla mas ma mtshon rtogs par mi nus so /
/ til brdungs phub ma bsal bar gyur pa las /
/ til mar snying po byung pa de bzhin du /
/ bla ma sten pas de bzhin [5a.3] de nyid don /
/ til mar bzhin du brda' yis bstan par bya /
/ yul rnams dbyer med ngo bo cig tu 'gyur /
/ kye ho ring 'gro gting dpag dka' ba'i don /[12]
/ da lta nyid du gsal ba ngo mtshar che /

/ ces (zhes) gsungs pas der 'dus pa thams cad grol bar gyur te / [5a.4] mgur de'i don bkrol ba / don la mi 'thun pa yang spang du med // gnyen po ye shes skyed du med // sa lam bsgrod du med // 'bras bu thob rgyu 'ang med // kun rdzob brda' tsam du bla mas stan dgos so // zhes pa'o // der khyed kyi bla ma su yin zhes [5a.5] pas

/ nga la mi'i bla ma yod /
/ klu sgrub tsarya la ba (wa) pa /
/ skal ba bzang mo bdag gi ni /
/ bka' babs bzhi'i bla ma yin /

/ zhes pas / klu sgrub la sgyu lus / tsarya pa la rmi lam / la wa pa la 'od gsal / mkha' 'gro ma la gtum mo zhus te snyan [5a.6] brgyud kyi chu bo chen po bzhi zhes grags so //

—1.2—

gNyis pa mkha' 'gro dbang du bsdus nas chos zhus pa ni // yang bud med rnams byung nas smras pa /

/ snyan rgyud yi ge med pa ni /
/ dri med mkha' 'gro ma la yod /
/ yid bzhin nor bu rnam gsum [5a.7] long /

/ zhes gsungs pas / ngas mi lon byas pas / yang bud med rnams 'di skad du

/ u rgyan gnas kyi ghando lir [*ghando-lar*] /
/ lung stan (bstan) dam tshig ldan pa yis /
/ skal ba can gyis blangs na lon /

/ ces (zhes) pas / ji ltar byas na lon byas pas / [5b.1] [[pas]] shel gyi skras pa dang / rin po che'i zam pa dang / rtsa byi zung rnams khyer la u rgyan du song ces [*zhes*] lung stan no [*lung-bstan-no*] // de rnams yab kyis tshegs med par snyed de (brnyes te) khyer nas phyin to //
de yang nub phyogs u rgyan gyi yul ghando la'i gtsug lag khang na chos [5b.2] sku ye shes kyi mkha' 'gro ma zhes bya ba de / dmigs pa chad pa med pa'i gnas na gnyis su med pa'i ngang la / bzhugs pa med pa'i tshul gyis rgyal mo'i[13] tshul du bzhugs so // de ka'i drung na long sku [*longs-sku*] rigs lnga'i mkha' 'gro ma [5b.3] {ma} bya ba de / rin po che'i pho brang na yid bzhin gyi nor bu rin po che rnam gsum ni rbas / mi phyed pa'i lcags kyis bcug ste rgya bdun gyis btab / mkhar dang 'obs dang lcags ris bskor nas blon po'i tshul du bzhugs so // de ka'i drung na sprul sku za byed [5b.4] las kyi mkha' 'gro ma de dad pa dang mos pa rnams la dngos sgrub [*dngos-grub*] ster / ma dad pa dang dam tshig nyams pa rnams tshar gcod cing za byed[14] / sgo ma'i tshul du bzhugs so // der bram ze'i khye'u des nub phyogs u rgyan gyi yul ghando li'i [*ghando-la'i*] gtsug lag khang gi [5b.5] drung du phyin pa dang / sprul skus [*sprul-sku*] las kyi mkha' 'gro ma ni sa chag pa [*sa-'chag-pa*] skad dam gnam gnam trum pa [*gnam-grum-pa?*] skad du

/ nga ni sprul sku las kyi mkha' 'gro ma /
/ mi'i sha la dga' zhing khrag la rngams /

zer nas byung pa dang bram ze'i khye'us

/ cher 'jigs mkha' [5b.6] 'gro du mas kyang /
/ nga'i ba spu'i rtse mi 'gul /

/ zhes gsungs nas / rig pa brtul zhugs kyi spyod pas zil gyis mnan te / lus mi g.yo ba / ngag mi rdzi ba / sems ma zhum pa'i lta stangs byas pas mkha' 'gro de rnams rgyal bar[15] [5b.7] gyur to / rgyal ba sangs pa dang smras pa /

/ kye ma mar mes sbrang ma rlag pa ltar /
/ khyod zar 'dod pas bdag cag phung /
/ dam pa bdag ni ci dgar mdzod /

/ zer ro // der bram ze'i khye'us nga nang du thong byas pas / mkha' 'gro rnams kyis [6a.1] smras pa

/ bdag cag dran [*bran*] ltar dbang chung pas /
/ blon mo dag la ma dris na /
/ bdag cag sha za khrag 'thung mchis /
/ dam pas nye bar dgongs par mdzod /

/ des longs sku'i mkha' 'gro ma la gtad do // de rnams na re / khyed [6a.2] brtul zhugs chungs 'dug pa nged kyis bsgral gyis yar thong cig gsung nas bram ze'i khye'us 'obs la rin po che'i zam pa btsugs / lcags ri la shel gyi skras pa btsugs / rtsa byi zungs kyi [*kyis*] sgo phye nas nang du phyin pa dang / blon mo rnams na re

/ 'jigs [6a.3] pa'i sku la 'jigs pa'i gsung /
/ 'jigs pa'i mtshon cha thogs nas kyang /
/ longs sku rigs lnga'i mkha' 'gro ma /
/ sha la dga' zhing khrag la rngam /

/ zhes zer ba dang / yang bram ze'i khye'us smras pa

/ cher 'jigs mkha' 'gro du mas[16] kyang
kho [6a.4] bo'i ba spu'i khung mi g.yo /

/ ces (zhes) brjod nas lta stangs byas pas rgyal bar gyur to // nga nang du thong byas pas / blon mos smras pa

/ bdag cag blon ltar dbang chung pas /
/ rgyal mo nyid la ma zhus na /
/ bdag cag bka' chad 'chad[17] [6a.5] pas gcod /
/ dam pas nye bar dgongs par mdzod /

/ zer te / chos sku'i mkha' 'gro la gsol ba btab nas khye'us nang du phyin pa dang / chos sku'i ye shes kyi mkha' 'gro la dpa' bo g.yas bral [gral] // dpa' mo g.yon bral [gral] la bsam [6a.6] gyis mi khyab pas bskor nas 'dug pas / bram ze'i khye'us phyag ma byas pas / 'khor de rnams na re

/ 'di ni sangs rgyas thams cad kyi /
/ yum gyur bcom ldan 'das ma la /
/ ma gus tshul can cis mi gzhom /

/ zer nas 'joms par [6a.7] rtsams pa dang / de'i dus su / chos sku'i mkha' 'gro ma'i zhal nas 'khor rnams la

/ 'di ni sangs rgyas thams cad kyi /
/ yab gyur bde mchog 'khor lo ste /
/ mkha' las rdo rje'i char phab kyang /
/ 'di tshe choms par ga la gyur /

/ ces (zhes) gsungs[18] [6b.1] pas / 'khor rnams kyis / rnam pa khye'u bde mchag 'khor lo [*bde-mchog-'khor-lo*] yin par ma shes pa'i tshul du smras pa / khyod sus btang / su yin / ci 'dod zer pas / bram ze'i khye'us smras pa

/ bdag ni paṇ tsa pa na yin /
/ sring mo bde ster ma [6b.2] yis btang /

/ lta spyod 'bras bu dam tshig dang /
/ sku gsum nor bu len du yongs (yong) /

/ byas pas / 'khor de dag gi khrel rgod bco [co] ba byas te / mgrin gcig tu smras pa

/ rmu long [*dmus-long*] bltas pas gzugs mi mthong /
/ 'on pas nyan pas sgra [6b.3] mi thos /
/ lkugs pas smras pas don mi go /
/ bdud kyis bslus la bden pa med /

/ ces zer ba la / yang slob dpon gyis smras pa /

/ nyes pa zad pa rdzun gyi tshig /
/ smra bar mi 'gyur rgyu med phyir /
/ bdud min [6b.4] mkha' 'gro ma ru bden /

/ byas pas de nas ye shes kyi mkha' 'gro mas sku tsa ka li / gsung yig 'bru / thugs phyag mtshan / nor bu rin po che'i brda' byung nas bram ze'i khye'us smras pa /

/ snang stong sku'i gsang mdzod nas /
/ mthun[19] mongs yid bzhin nor bu zhu /
/ brjod bral gsung gi gsang mdzod nas /
/ dam tshig [6b.5] yid bzhin nor bu zhu /
/ rtog med thugs kyi gsang mdzod nas /
/ gnas lugs yid bzhin nor bu zhu /

/ byas pas / ye shes kyi mkha' 'gro mas smras pa /

/ thun mongs yid bzhin nor bu la /
/ lung bstan nyams kyi lde mig dgos /
/ lung ma bstan [6b.6] pas phyed [*'byed*] mi 'gyur /
/ dam tshig yid bzhin nor bu la /
/ bka' rgyud zab mo'i lde mig dgos /
/ gnyen po med pas phyed [*'byed*] mi 'gyur /
/ gnas lugs yid bzhin nor bu la /

/ shes rab zab mo'i lde mig dgos /
/ rtogs pa [6b.7] med pas phyed [*'byed*] mi 'gyur /

/ ces (zhes) gsungs[20] pa dang / bram ze'i khye'us smras pa

/ mkha' 'gro'i gsang tshig thugs kyi (kyis) sdom /
/ ma rig mun sel ye shes sgron /
/ rang rig rang byung rang gsal gyi /
/ lung bstan nyams kyi lde mig yod /
/ gang [7a.1] yang skye ba med pa yi /
/ sems nyid rang grol chos sku la /
/ rang grol phyag rgya chen por shar /
/ dam tshig rang grol lde mig yod /
/ dmigs pa yid la mi byed cing /
/ dran pa rdul tsam ma skyes pa'i /
/ sems nyid [7a.2] chos nyid chos sku la /
/ mthong pa nyams kyi lde mig yod /

/ ces smras pa dang / ye shes kyi mkha' 'gro'i longs sprul gnyis kyis ram bu steg te [*ste*] mgrin gcig tu / mgur[21] 'di bzhes pa /

/ bdag cag yab gcig bcom ldan 'das /
/ [7a.3] te lo sangs rgyas 'gro ba'i mgon /
/ 'khor lo bde mchog bde ba che /
/ yid bzhin nor bu rnam gsum 'bul /

/ gsungs nas rtsa rgyud le'u nga gcig pa bshad rgyud dang bcas pa dang snyan rgyud gnang ngo // de ye shes kyi mkha' 'gro ma'i zhal nas / nga'i [7a.4] sku sgrub par 'dod na bskyed rims la brtson par gyis shig / gsung snying po la thugs rdzogs rims phyag rgya chen po la brtson par gyis shig / gtsug gi nor bu'i dgon par song la / na ro ri ri ka so ri gsum brjes su [*rjes-su*] zung shig /

gsungs nas gtso mo [7a.5] mi snang par gyur to // mtshan te lo shes rab bzang por btags so // smras pa

/ kho bos mkha' la bya bzhin du /
/ 'od gsal sems kyi bya 'phur nas /
/ thog med [*thogs-med*] shes rab bzang po 'gro /

/ byas pas / longs sprul gnyis kyi mkha' 'gros smras pa

/ [7a.6] dam pa khyod ni ji lta bu /
/ bdag cag don du bzhugs par zhu /

/ zhes zhus pas / te los smras pa

/ gtso mo nyid kyi lung bstan ltar /
/ snod ldan don du rnal 'byor bdag /
/ gtsug gi nor bu'i dgon par 'gro /

/ gsungs nas byon pa'i lam [7a.7] du / lus med mkha' 'gro'i chos skor dgu bar snang nas gnang pa ni

/ lus med mkha' 'gro'i rdo rje'i gsuṇg /
/ dri za'i glu dbyangs snyan pa ltar /
/ bar snang stong las 'di ltar thos /

/ smin grol sems kyi rgya mdud bshig /
/ dam tshig rang sems me long ltos /
/ [7b.1] rtsa rlung gra mig 'khor lo bskor /
/ bde chen gsung gi rin chen zung /
/ rig pa ye shes sgron me ltos /
/ rang grol phyag rgya chen po ltos /
/ dam rdzas rtogs pa'i nyi ma lde /
/ spyod pa chu la ral gri rgyob /
/ ro snyoms phyi'i me long ltos /

/ shes (zhes) pa de rnams bar snang las [7b.2] gsan nas / te los smṛas pa

/ gtso mo ji lta'i tshul ston te /
/ sgyu ma lus kyi ghan do lar /
/ lus med mkha' 'gro'i gsang bcug nas /
/ brjod med ngag gis lcags bcug ste /
/ 'od gsal sems kyi bya 'phur 'gro /

/ gsungs nas gtsug gi [7b.3] nar bu'i [*gtsug-gi nor-bu'i*] dgon pa a ḍo na'i gcug [gtsug] lag khang du [*gtsug-lag-khang-du*] gshegs so //

—1.3—

gSum pa mi'i bla ma med pa ni / der mi mang po 'tshogs nas grub pa thob nas ghando la nas chos lon yod gda' ba / bla ma su yin zer ba la

/ nga la mi'i bla ma [7b.4] mad [*med*] /
/ bla ma thams cad mkhyen pa yin /

/ ces (zhes) gsungs pa'o //

—1.4—

bZhi pa sprul pa sna tshogs bstan pa ni / brgyad ste [*de*] / dang po rnal 'byor pa zil gyis mnan pa dang / mu stegs pa / sgyu ma mkhan / chang 'tshong ma / glu mkhan / bshan pa / las 'bras med [7b.5] par smra ba mthu bo che brtul (btul) ba'o //

—1.4.1—

Dang po ni / rgya gar lho phyogs na rgyal po gcig la ma shin tu byams pas ma de gang dgyes pa byed pas / dge rtsa gang la dga' / dge ba gcig bya yis bka' gsol byas pas / ma na re / paṇḍita dang / [7b.6] grub thob dang / mkha' 'gro ma bsags te rin po che'i dkyil 'khor bar snang la bzhengs nas dbang bskur chen po dang tshogs kyi 'khor lo byed na dga' zer nas / de ltar byed pa'i paṇḍita rnams la bang chen re btang / grub thob rnams la bang chen gcig btang [7b.7] nas / paṇḍita dang grub thob rnams spyan drangs te / paṇḍitas sa chog la sogs pa mdzad pas / 'di rnams kyis gang mdzad kyang yong zhes bsgrags / ku sa li rnams kyis mdun du bud med mi sdug pa'i msthan ma can gcig 'ongs nas / khyed kyi tshogs [8a.1] [[tshogs]] dpon sus byed zer ba la / 'dran zla med pas [*'gran-zla-med-pa*] ngas byed gsungs pas / khyod kyis mi 'ong / nga'i ming pos 'ong ste byas pas ga na yod zer ba la dur khrod na yod byas pas / 'o na khug la shog zer nas / [8a.2] 'gugs su song pas yong par yod kyis zer / der 'chi mo [*phyi-mo*] na byon nas khri gnyis la 'dran zla med pa [*'gran-zla-med-pa*][22] dang gcig bzhugs te / sgra dang don gyi 'gal 'grel ston pa'i tshad ma la brtsad pas mnyam par byung / nam kha' [mkha'] la dkyil 'khor 'bri ba dang / [8a.3] char dang rlung gis mi snang par bya ba'i re mos byas pas snyam par byung [*mnyam-par byung*] / seng ge la zhon nyi zla'i khar bang btang pas yang mnyam par byung pa la / te los nyi zla thang la dbab / de'i steng du seng ge zhon / lus phyir bzlog / ba spu nyag re la [8a.4] dkyil 'khor dur khrod bcas pa re sprul / der shing re sprul / shing re la dkyil dkrungs bcas pa rtsed mo byas pas / 'dran zla med [*'gran-zla-med*] ma byung pas[23] / thams cad ngo mtshar te / e ma 'di lta bu'i rdzu 'phrul ci las byung

/ ngo mtshar spyod pa ci las byung /

ces (zhes) brjod [8a.5] pas / lan mgur du bzhes pa

/ kye ma 'dug na nam kha'i (mkha'i) dkyil du 'dug /
/ nyal na mdung gi rtse la nyal /
/ lta na nyi zla'i dkyil du ltos /

/ don dam rtogs pa'i te lo pa /
/ nga ni 'bad rtsol kun dang bral /

/ ces (zhes) pa dang rang bzhin bsam [8a.6] gyis mi khyab pa gsungs pas / thams cad grol bar gyur to // mtshan yang nus ldan blo gros zhes bya bar btags te / da lta yang u rgyan na 'das grongs mi mnga' bar bzhugs so //

—1.4.2—

gNyis pa mu stegs pa btul [8a.7] ba ni / dpal shri na len trar [*nā-lan-dār*] / mu stegs pa'i ston pa grub thob gcig yod pa la / phyi nang thams cad rngun [*rgyun*?] ldang bya dgos ma byas na nus pa dang brtsod pa [*brtsad-pa*] 'gran dgos pa la / te lo pas ldang ba ma byas pas / khyod nga la nus pa dang brtsod pa [*brtsad-pa*] [8b.1] bdo' ba [*bdo-ba*] gcig 'dug pas 'dran [*'gran*] zer nas / rgyal po dgung la bzhag / phyi nang gi paṇḍita thams cad 'tshogs nas gang rgyal ba'i bstan pa la 'jug par bya ste brtsod pas [*brtsad-pas*] kyang mu stegs pa pham par byas / nus pa 'dran pas [*'gran-pas*] kyang te lo pa ma thub nas / [8b.2] mu stegs pas kha nas me phyung nas btang pas

/ khams gsum kun kyang g.yo byed pa'i /
/ nga yis mi 'jigs su zhig yin /

/ zer bas / phar log nas lan mgur du bzhes pa /

/ blta na rmu long [*dmus-long*] mig gis ltos /
/ skom na mig rgyu'i [*smig-rgyu'i*] [8b.3] chu la 'thung /
/ bying na bum pa rlung gis khengs /
/ 'jigs pa kun bral te lo yin /

/ ces (zhes) pa dang / chos nyid bsam gyis mi khyab pa gsungs pas thams cad grol bar gyur to // mtshan yang nag po dge ba zhes btags te / [8b.4] da lta yang sil ba'i tshal na 'das grongs med par bzhugs so //

—1.4.3—

gSum pa / sgyu ma mkhan btul ba la / sgyu ma mkhan gcig gis sgyu ma'i dmag gis rgyal po'i yul 'don pa la / bud med mi sdug pa'i mtshan ma can gcig [8b.5] yongs (yong) nas / khyod kyi dmag dpon gang gis byed byas pas 'di dang 'dis byed byas pas / des mi yong nga'i ming pos yong pa yin te byas pas / ming po gang na yod byas pas dur khrod na shing sha ba dpag tshad gcig la rta rnga btags / de la mi ro'i rkang pa rtag [*btags*] / de'i lag pa la yang rta lnga rtag ste [*btags-te*][24] / de la [8b.6] 'jus nas gar byed cing yod // zer / rgyal po la snyad pas rgyal po na re / bud med de la mi srid pa'i gtam gsum byung pas de khrid la shog gsung nas dris pas / gong gi kho na zer te / ltar btang pas mo zer ba bzhin 'dug nas / de nas te lo [8b.7] pa spyan drangs te / sgyu mar ma shes te shor la khad pa la sgyu ma bshig / 'ga' zhig bsad sgyu ma mkhan bzung pa las / sgyu ma mkhan na re

/ chos la rten pa'i skyes bu khyod
de ltar bsod pa mngag ma (ga la) rigs /

/ zer bas / [9a.1] lan mgur du bzhes pa

/ sgyu ma'i dmag tshogs bsad pa la /
/ sems med phyir na sdig pa med /
/ bsod na sgyu ma'i[25] skyes bu bsod /
/ sgom na dbugs bral lta bur bsgoms /
/ smra na lkugs pa'i lce yis[26] [9a.2] smros /
/ 'dod na yi ge zad par skyol /

/ ces (zhes) pa dang dngos po bsam gyis mi khyab pa gsungs pas thams cad grol bar gyur to // mtshan yang slu byed bden smra zhes btags te / da lta yang ha ha sgrog pa na 'das grongs med par bzhugs [9a.3] [[bzhugs]] so //

—1.4.4—

bZhi pa 'chang 'tshong ma btul ba ni / 'chang 'tshong ma gcig 'chang 'tshong pa'i dus su / te los sprul pa'i spre'u dang byi las chang btsags kyin 'thungs pas mos ngus pas / mi rnams ci nyes zer lo rgyus[27] snyad [9a.4] pas / mi rnams na re / rnal 'byor pa de rang la gsol ba thob dang zer bas chang mas ngus te

/ bdag gi mtsho [*'tsho*] ba chad pas na /
/ thugs rje (rjes) rjes su bzung du gsol /

/ zhes pas / skad gcig (cig) la chang rdza thams cad chang gis gang par byas ste [*te*] / mgur bzhes [9a.5] pa

/ skom na dug chu khol ma 'thung /
/ 'phro na spre'u ded la sod /
/ gnyen po sgom chen byi la rten (bsten) /
/ thams cad lhan skyes ro ru bsgyur /
/ don dam sprang po te lo pa /
/ khyod kyis mthong med rnal 'byor yin /

/ ces (zhes) pa dang bsam gyis [9a.6] mi khyab pa'i bde ba chen po gsungs pas thams cad grol bar gyur to // mtshan yang nyi 'od sgron mar btags te / da lta yang so sa gling na 'das 'grongs med par bzhugs so //

—1.4.5—

lNga pa glu mkhan btul ba / glu mkhan mkhas [9a.7] pa gcig yod pas / de'i drung du te lo pas bsam glu blangs pas / khyod 'gran nam zer 'gran gyis byas ste [*te*] slob dpon gyis glu long zhig / de nas nga yis blang gi gsungs pas / khos kyang rdzogs rdzogs blangs nas de nas slob dpon gyis blangs pas / [9b.1] rdzogs pa ma byung pas khos ma thub / kho na re

/ nga ni tshangs pa'i 'jig rten yang
skyong par [*skyeng-par*] byed pa'i glu mkhan yin /

/ zer bas / lan du mgur bzhes pa

/ skyo na dri za'i grong khyer ltos /
/ nyan na bung ba'i glu la nyon /
/ lta na [9b.2] rmu long [*dmus-long*] mig gis ltos /
/ thos yul rnams ni drag cha [*brag-cha*] 'dra /

/ ces (zhes) pa dang rol mo bsam gyis mi khyab pa gsungs pas / thams cad grol bar gyur to // mtshan yang dbyangs ldan lkugs pa zhes btags te / da lta yang na ga ra na 'das [9b.3] 'grongs yod [*med*] par bzhugs so //

—1.4.6—

Drug pa shan pa btul ba ni / shan pa gcig sems can gyi bu tsha thams cad bsad nas bu gcig bso ba [*gso-ba*] / sha btsos te bu la sbyin snyam nas khog ma kha phye bas / te los bu'i rkang lag [9b.4] (rong)yong par sprul pas / kho na re

/ rang gis byas pa'i sdig pa de /
/ rang la 'khor ram ji ltar yin /

/ zer nas mya ngan gyis gdungs pa la 'o na gzhan[28] mi bsod na khyod rang gi bu yong pa bya yis gsungs pas / mi [9b.5] bsod [*bsad*] zer bas / lan mgur du

/ 'byed na mar khu dangs (dvangs) snyings 'byed /
/ sreg na dus mtha' me yis sregs /
/ 'don na rlung sems[29] spyi bor thon /
/ 'khrud na sems kyi dri ma khrus /

/ ces (zhes) pa dang bsod pa'i [*gsod-pa'i*] sbyor ba bsam gyis mi khyab pa [9b.6] gsungs pas thams cad grol bar gyur to // mtshan yang bde byed dga' ba zhes btags so //

da lta yang srin po'i gling na 'das 'grongs mi mnga' bar bzhugs so //

—1.4.7—

bDun pa / las 'bras med par 'dod pa btul ba ni / rgyu 'bras la bkur [9b.7] pa 'debs pa'i rgyang phan pa las dge sdig med zer / nang pa sangs rgyas pas yod zer brtsod pa'i [*brtsad-pa'i*] dpang po slob dpon la bcol bas / slob dpon gyis las rgyu 'bras yod par 'dod pa rgyal ces (zhes) gsungs pas / rgyang phan pa na re / dngos su mthong ba [10a.1] med zer ba la / slob dpon gyis kho khrid de lha dang dmyal ba la sogs pa thams cad sprul gyis bstan nas / lha gnas gcig na lha mo zla med gcig 'dug pa la ci yin byas pas / mu stegs pa 'ga' zhig gis dge ba byed pa yod pas / [10a.2] de'i zla rogs byed pa yin zer / yang dmyal bar khrid nas phyin pa dang / zangs re re'i nang na gtso rgyu re 'dug pa la gcig na mi 'dug nas / 'dir ci 'tshod byas pas mu stegs pa las dge sdig med zer ba kun 'dir 'tshod zer bas bred 'dug skad / [10a.3] khos smras pa

/ las kyis bsags pa'i sdig pa yi /
/ dmyal ba rang gi sems la 'khor /
/ las kyis bsags pa'i dge ba yis /
/ mtho ris rang gi sems la 'khor /

/ zer bas / lan mgur du

/ chags na dur khrod gling du skyol /
/ rgud na rgyal mtshan [10a.4] rtse la phyogs /
/ rnam par rtog pa sprul sku ste /
/ ngas ni bstan pa ci yang med /

/ ces dang / sna tshogs bsam gyis mi khyab pa gsungs pas thams cad grol bar gyur to // mtshan yang dzi na byang

chub zhes btags te / da lta yang dpal gyi ri [10a.5] la 'das 'grongs med par bzhugs so //
gzhan yang lus kyi bkod pas sdig mkhan la chos bshad / bzo bo gzo mkhas pa [*bzo-mkhas-pa*] / sgom chen pa grub pa po / de ltar nya pa dang / khyi ra pa (ba) la sogs pa dpag tu med pa bstan pas / [10a.6] de rnams kyis smras pa /

nya pa la sogs pa byed pa

zer bas

/ don dam rtogs pa'i te lo pa /
/ dge sdig zhes bya'i ming yang med /

/ zer nas gdams ngag zhus so //

—1.4.8—

brGyad pa / mthu mkhan btul ba ni / mthu mkhan gcig gis mthu byas nas thams cad [10a.7] bsod pas [*bsad-pas*] de 'dul ba'i dus la bab par gzigs nas / te lo dang gnyis chad [*bcad*] 'gran pas mnyam por byas tshad shi ba la te los shi tshad blangs / bud mad [*bud-med*] la sogs pa 'ga' zhig ma blangs / kho rang kyang (yang) sdong po rgad po 'dra ba gcig byas [10b.1] nas / da khyod kyi bu mad [*bud-med*] slongs na mthu mi byed dam gsungs pas / khos ma bsos te smras pa

/ sos pa med pa'i spyod pa 'di /
/ shan pa rang dang khyad med dam /

/ zer bas / lan mgur du bzhes pa

/ ltos cig rang gi sems la bltos /
/ [10b.2] snang pa'i ri bo khyur mid kyis /
/ rgya mtsho chen po hub kyis thob /
/ 'khor ba'i ltos thag chod la zhog /

/ ces pa dang / 'phrin las bsam gyis mi khyab pa gsungs pas / thams cad grol bar gyur to // mtshan yang nyi i mi zhes [10b.3] btags te / da lta yang gnas ki mi tsi ki li na bzhugs so //

—2—

sPyi don gnyis pa / bde mchog gi sprul par bstan pa ni / rgya gar shar phyogs na du ka ta'i 'gram / chu bo kha su'i rtsa / dur khrod rma sha'i tshal / dgon pa mya ngan med pa bya [10b.4] ba yod / de na ti lo pa'i zhang po dang ma btsun ma yin pas mkhan slob byas nas / der rab tu byung ste dge slong ka la par btags so // gzhan rnams 'khor gsum la zhugs la / khong chos spyod mi byed par cha ga ba mang po bsad cing [10b.5] mgo phyogs gcig bstan / lus phyogs gcig tu bstan pas kun gyis 'phya ba la zhugs so // de yang dge dgos la [*dge-skos-la*] gnyer yod pas gros thob byas ste [*te*] / dge bkos kyis [*dge-skos-kyis*] spyir chos pa dgos [*sgos*] btsun pa yang dgos [*sgos*] mya ngan med pa'i bla 'tshogs [10b.6] byas nas zhes rgal ba [*brgal-ba*] dang / yul de'i rgyal pos smras pa /

/ btsun gzugs srog chags bsod pa [*bsad-pa*] khyod /
/ yul dang mkhan slob su zhig yin /

/ ces (zhes) dris pas / lan mgur du gsungs pa

/ dgon pa mya ngan med pa yin /
/ [10b.7] mkhan slob ma dang zhang po yin /
/ bdag rang dga slong [*dge-slong*] te lo yin /
/ nga yis skal pa bye ba ru /
/ zhing khams brgya ru nga yis phyin /
/ klu sgrub arya de wa [*ārya-de-wa*] dang /
/ sangs rgyas rnams dang nga gtam byas /
/ ngas ni sangs rgyas stong yang mthong /
/ [11a.1] ngas ni sems can bsad pa med /

/ ces gsungs pa dang / cha ga rnams sbrid di re 'phur song skad / thams cad yid ches te bde mchog gi sprul par grags so //

—3—

gSum pa bde mchog dngos su 'dod pa ni / rgya gar shar phyogs su [11a.2] bsod snyoms la byon pas / phar la 'gro tsa na gom pa babs kyis 'dor[30] / mig gnya' shing gang du lta / snyan sngags kyi tshig bcad [*tshigs-bcad*] 'don / tshur 'byon tsa na sbyin len gyi shis pa brjod pas / mi rnams mos nas yod pa la / yul de'i [11a.3] rgyal pos thams cad spyan drangs te / mnyen bkur nas [*bsnyen-bkur-nas*] rgyal pos sgra mkhan rnams kyi sgra dang mi 'gal bar / de bzhin du tshad ma dang / lung dang / man ngag dang / nyams myong dang / rtog pa can rnams kyi rtogs pa dang mi 'gal ba'i sbyin len [11a.4] gyi tshigs su bcad pa re thon cig / byas ste [*te*] thams cad kyis ston pas [*bstan-pas*] phyogs re re gnyis gnyis dang mi 'gal bar byung / slob dpon gyis res la bab nas bton pas / thams cad dang mi 'gal zhing de dang de'i don mthar thug par byung nas rgyal pos bris pas

/ bdag la [11a.5] pha ma ma mchis te /
/ 'khor lo bde mchog bde ba'i mchog /
/ bdag la mkhan slob ma[31] mchis te /
/ bdag ni rang byung sangs rgyas yin /
/ bdag la sgra tshad ma mchis te /
/ gtan tshigs rig pa rang brdol yin /
/ bde mchog [11a.6] sku gsung thugs dang ni /
/ lus ngag yid gsum dbye ru med /
/ nga ni bde ba chen por 'gro /

/ ces (zhes) gsungs pas bde mchog dngos su grags so //

—4—

bZhi pa dus gsum gyi sangs rgyas thams cad kyi sku 'dus par bstan pa ni / [11a.7] rgyal po seng ge zla bas grub thob mang po spyan drangs nas gnyen bskur nas [*bsnyen-bkur-nas*] dbang bskur zhu ba la / te lo pas bar snang la rdul tshon gyi dkyil 'khor bzhengs pas mthong snang mi gcig pa la / te los mgur bzhes pa

/ bdag lus kye kye'i [11b.1] rdo rje la /
/ ngag ni ma hā ma ya yin /
/ sems ni bde mchog 'khor lo ste /
/ phung khams gsang ba 'dus pa la /
/ yan lag nag po sgra rgyud nyid /
/ nying lag rdo rje 'jigs byed la /
/ bas spu [*ba-spu*] dus gsum sangs rgyas yin /

/ ces (zhes) gsungs pas / [11b.2] te lo pa de sangs rgyas thams cad 'dus pa'i skur grags so //

de lta bu'i mdzad pa tha (mtha') mas shar phyogs za hor gyi 'gro ba rnams smin grol la[32] bkod de / grong khyer 'bum tsho bdun stongs par gyur to //
de nas grub pa thob pas kyang sprul pa'i [11b.3] skur grags pa / rnal 'byor gyi dbang phyug[33] te lo pa'i lo brgyus [*lo-rgyus*] / sku che ba'i yon tan de nyid kyis mdzad pa'i gzhung rang mtshan du byas nas mtha' dag pa zhig bstan zin //

dpal gro bo lung gi dgon par / sras mdo [11b.4] sde'i don du yi ger bkod pa rdzogs so // maṅ ga laṃ //

Translation of the Tibetan Text

—0—

[1b] Beyond any formulation, pervading throughout space, with the nine features of dance[1]—three are the Bodies (Tib. *sku*, Skt. *kāya*) that ripen the devotee: a vast sea [comes] from them, not even slightly defective, the waves of which are the Ḍākinīs of the[se] three pure Bodies.

A lotus sprung from [these] waters—the Great Bliss (Tib. *bde-chen*, Skt. *mahāsukha*)—is the result of the actual manifestations as Prajñābhadra (*Shes-rab-bzang-po*),[2] the Protector of beings (Tib. *'Gro-mngon*, Skt. *Jagannātha*), and as Nāropa mahāpaṇḍita (*paṇ-chen*) who endured twelve [years] of hardships: to them I pay homage!

/ gang zhig sku gsum nor bu la /
The Gem of the three Bodies:
/ gang gis mi shes rgyas gdab pa /
[To] those who seal [it] out of ignorance,
/ mkha' 'gro'i gsang tshig lde mig gi /
This key of the Ḍākinīs' secret words,
/ rnam gsum nor bu rab tu stan bya'o /
[2a] This threefold Gem, shall be thoroughly shown.

/ ngo sprod yid bzhin nor bu yis /
Through the Wish-Fulfilling Gem (*cintāmaṇi*) of the introduction,
/ chos kyi sku la ngo sprod bya /
The Dharmakāya is to be introduced;
/ rmi lam yid bzhin nor bu yis /
Through the Wish-Fulfilling Gem of the dream state,

/ longs sku lus la bzhug par bya /
The Sambhogakāya is to enter the body;
/ brgyud pa yid bzhin nor bu yis /
Through the Wish-Fulfilling Gem of the transmission,
/ chos sku dngos su stan par bya'o /
The Dharmakāya is to be shown in its actual existence.

/ mkha' 'gro'i snyan brgyud nyi ma'i 'od gsal la /
At the sunlight of the Ḍākinīs' oral transmission (*karṇa-tantra*),
/ lha min sgra gcan brjod pas rab 'jigs nas /
Rāhu, the Asura, is terrified by [their] pronouncement; so,
/ mdo sde'i don phyir yi ger bkod pa la /
In order to compose [it] for [my son] mDo-sde,
/ mkha' 'gros bzod gsol byin gyis rlobs /
May the Ḍākinīs forgive and bless[3] [me]!

/ snyan brgyud gdam pa kun la stan pa min /
The instruction (*upadeśa*) of the[ir] oral transmission is not a teaching for everybody:
/ ltogs kyang pha ma'i sha la bza' ba min /
Even if hungry, one will not eat [his] parents' flesh;
/ khe'ang btsan dug sbyar ba 'tshong ba min /
Even if profitable, one will not sell a thing mixed with a strong poison;
/ ltad mo che'ang rang gi snying sprul ston pa min /
Even if it is a wonderful show, one will not display his own heart.

Now, in the Ḍākinīs' oral transmission, [2b] this wonderful one, there are three [divisions]: (1) the characteristics of the teacher who teaches, (2) the characteristics of the disciple who is to be taught, and (3) the actual being of Dharma (*chos*) which is to be taught. As for the first one, it is the one who possesses an accomplished transmission with compassion and so forth. As for the second one, it is the one who has the potential for attaining the [state of] Buddha (*Sangs-rgyas*) in this transmission, in one life, one body, and so forth. As for the third one, the actual being of Dharma which is to be taught, it has three [divisions]: the outer one is the Wish-Fulfilling Gem of the transmission, [that is] the instruction of the Nirmāṇakāya subjugating doubts; the inner one is the Wish-Fulfilling Gem of the Developing Path (Tib. *smin-lam*, Skt. *vipākamārga*), [that is] the instruction of the Sambhogakāya concerning the practice; the secret one is the Wish-Fulfilling Gem of the Liberation Path (Tib. *grol-lam*, Skt. *muktimārga*), [that is] the instruction of the Dharmakāya [by which] it is introduced.

Out of them, this is the Wish-Fulfilling Gem of transmission of the instruction of the Nirmāṇakāya. The account of the Jñanaḍākinī (*Ye-shes-kyi mkha'-'gro-ma*) as the Dharmakāya and of the siddhas' lineage as the Nirmāṇakāya are both in it. As for the first one, it will be explained in detail later how this [3a] Jñanaḍākinī entering the three Bodies is like all Buddhas entering the three Bodies. As for the second, among the [accounts of the] perfect liberation (*rnam-thar*) of the siddhas' lineage of the Nirmāṇakāya, at the outset, in the perfect liberation of Tilopa, there are four [sections]: his fame (1) as a human being, (2) as a manifestation of Cakrasaṃvara (*bDe-mchog*),[4] (3) as Cakrasaṃvara himself, and (4) as the synthesis of the Bodies of all Buddhas (*Sangs-rgyas thams-cad-kyi sku 'dus-pa*).

—1—

As for the first [section,] the human lineage of this great lord Tilopa has four great qualities. They are, with respect to the interpretative meaning (Tib. *drang-don,* Skt. *neyārtha*): (1) he was prophesied by the Ḍākinī, looked for a guru and practised until the accomplishment; (2) he outshone the Ḍākinīs and asked [them] for the Dharma. With respect to the definitive meaning (Tib. *nges-don,* Skt. *nītārtha*),[5] he showed himself (3) as one without human gurus, and (4) under several manifestations.

—1.1—

Here is the first [chapter] concerning Tilopa. The father was the brāhmaṇa gSal-ba, the mother was the brāhmaṇī gSal-ldan-ma, and the sister was the brāhmaṇī gSal-ba'i sGron-ma. These three lived in a city called Jago, in the country of Sahor in East India.[6] Since no son had come yet, they worshipped all the sacred receptacles, both outer and inner ones, with offerings and prayers. Eventually a son was born and, at that moment, a light (Tib. *'od,* Skt. *prabhā*) pervaded East India: because of that, he was given the name Prabhāsvara (*gSal-'od*). Then, a brāhmaṇa sooth-sayer [3b] was sought, and he spoke thus:

/ 'di ni lha klu gnod sbyin nam /
As for him, whether a Deva, a Nāga, a Yakṣa, or
/ sangs rgyas gang yin ma 'tshal bas /
Whether a Buddha, I do not understand what he is.
/ skyes bu mchog 'di gces par skyongs /
Anyhow, protect this supreme being with care![7]

Good care was taken care of the boy accordingly. But once, while [his] father was out and the two, mother and son, were alone, a glimmering vision appeared. [The mother] looked at it. Many women had come into view, bearing the signs of ugliness, blowing from their mouths, lame and walking with the support of sticks. As the mother was wondering if they were devils and whether her child would die, those women spoke:

/ gces par bskyangs kyang mi 'chi ba'i /
Even if you nourish him with care, a deathless
/ sa phyogs dag kyang yod ma yin /
Place does not exist anywhere![8]

Then the mother asked: "In that case, what is to be done for [his] benefit?" At that they spoke again: "O child!"

/ ma he skyong zhing yi ge slobs /
Herd buffalo and learn scriptures.
/ mkha' 'gro ma yi lung bstan 'byung /
The prophecy of the Ḍākinī will come![9]

Having said that, they disappeared.

Then, when he was grown up, he was allowed to act accordingly. While he was herding buffalo, the same women as before appeared [to him] and asked about his country, his parents, and so forth. The boy said to them in reply:

/ yul ni shar phyogs dza ko yin /
My country is Jago, in the East,
/ pha ni bram ze gsal ba yin /
My father is the brāhmaṇa gSal-ba,
/ ma ni bram ze gsal ldan yin /
My mother is the brāhmaṇī [4a] gSal-ldan-ma,
/ sring mo bram ze gsal sgron yin /
My sister is the brāhmaṇī gSal-sgron,
/ nga rang bram ze gsal 'od yin /
I am the brāhmaṇa Prabhāsvara,
/ shing 'di sha ba'i sdong po yin /
This tree is an Aloes-wood.[10]

/ yi ge bslabs nas dam chos byed /
Having learned the scriptures, I will practise Dharma;
/ ma he nor phyir skyong pa yin /
I herd buffalo to earn my living.[11]

So he said, and those women, pretending to be angry with him, replied: "O boy, you do not know it!"

/ yul ni nub phyogs u rgyan yin /
Your country is Uḍḍiyāṇa,[12] in the West,
/ yab ni bde mchog 'khor lo yin /
Your father is Cakrasaṃvara,
/ yum ni rdo rje phag mo yin /
Your mother is Vajravarāhī,[13]
/ sring mo mkha' 'gro bde ster ma /
Your sister is [me,] Sukhadā,
/ khyod rang paṇ tsa pa na yin /
You are Pañcapana.
/ 'dud 'gro ma he ma skyong por /
Do not herd buffalo, the animals:
/ byang chub shing gi nags khrod du /
In the forest of the Bodhi-tree (*bodhivṛkṣa*)
/ nyams myong ma he rgyun du skyongs /
Herd always the buffalo of experience (*anubhava*)![14]

In response, the boy spoke: "I do not know how to do that!" Then he was instructed: "Go to the cemetery of Sālavihāra:[15] [there] it will be shown [to you]."

There is a cemetery called Sālavihāra in the South, which had been blessed by Maheśvara (*dBang-phyug-chen-po*). That son of brāhmaṇa arrived there while a gaṇacakra (*tshogs-kyi 'khor-lo*) of outer and inner Ḍākinīs was being performed, and received the instructions from Cāryapa (*Tsarya-pa*).[16]

The great teacher Lavapa (*La-wa-pa*)[17] sang:

/ grong khyer chen po'i srang mdo ru /
At the street corner of a great town,
/ bcu gnyis bar du gnyid log pas /
I had been sleeping for twelve years when
/ phyag rgya chen po'i dngos grub thob /
I attained the perfection (*siddhi*) of the Great Seal (*mahāmudrā*)!

[From Lavapa] he received the instruction of the radiant light (Tib. *'od-gsal*, Skt. *prabhāsvara*). Then, in the cemetery, where he was looking for Nāgārjuna (*Klu-sgrub*),[18] Mātaṅgīpa (*Ma-tang-gi*), a yogin practitioner of ascetic penance (Tib. *brtul-zhugs*, Skt. *vrata*), was meditating in a hut: "O boy!" he said. "Nāgārjuna went to explain the Dharma to the king of Gandharvas (*dri-za*), so he sent me to take care of you." There, he offered maṇḍalas to him and requested the instruction. [In response] he manifested the actual maṇḍala of Śrīguhya-samāja (*dPal-gsang-ba-'dus-pa'i dkyil-'khor dngos-su sprul*) and gave the empowerment (Tib. *dbang-bskur*, Skt. *abhiṣeka*).[19] Then, by means of the explanation of its tantra,[20] he perceived the reality of thinking activity (Tib. *sems-kyi ngo-bo*, Skt. *cittasvabhāva*).

In a temple where his uncle was accustomed to read the *Śatasāhasrikā*,[21] a woman[22] appeared and asked him, "Do you understand its meaning?" "I do not," he answered. She said, [4b] "Well, I will explain it!" and she explained the meaning of that [text]. Then, she gave him the empowerment of Hevajra (*He-badzra*) and Cakrasaṃvara (*'Khor-lo-sdom-pa*), and explained their tantras.[23] Then she said: "This is the view of Luipa (*Lu-hi-pa*), you must meditate on it." "But my uncle does not let me meditate," he said. "Fasten the *Śatasāhasrikā* with a rope, throw it from the door of the temple into the water, act like a madman: meditate in this way! My blessings will prevent the *Śatasāhasrikā* from being damaged," she said, and he did as he was told. The *Śatasāhasrikā* remained undamaged, but he was scolded as a madman and was beaten. He then practised, inseparable with Sugatas' Mind (*bDe-bar-gshegs-pa'i thugs gnyis-su-med-pa*), the two Stages.[24] After some time, he was instructed:

/ shar phyogs bhang ga la'i brgyud /
In Bengal, in the East,
/ paṇ tsha pa na'i tshong 'dus na /
In the market-place of Pañcapana,
/ smad 'tshong bha ri 'khor bcas kyi /
There is the prostitute Bharima and her retinue.
/ de yi zhabs 'breng byas na gsangs /
If you follow it as her servant, you will be purified;
/ spyod mthar thon nas dngos grub thob /
You will pass over the limits of practice and attain perfection!

He went there according to what she had said. Then, in the night-time he would do the work of inviting and accompanying men [into Bharima's]. During the day, he worked at thrashing sesame grains, and that is why he was known as Tilopa in the language of India[25] and, in Tibetan, as the Sesame-watcher (*Til-bsrungs-zhabs*). After that, he and Bharima went to the cemetery called Ke-re-li. There they took delight in the practice of the secret mantra (*gsang-ba-sngags*) and performed it to its completion.

Once again, while thrashing the remaining sesame grains in a market-place, he attained the perfection close to the sublime Great Seal. At that moment, the people of the town had different visions of him: some saw flames blazing from him, while others saw his ornaments of bones blazing. The people asked for instruction. At this he said: "O devotees, may this inborn reality in my mind (Tib. *yid,* Skt. *manas*) enter your hearts!" Immediately they were liberated.

Then, as the king of that country, surrounded by his retinue, came on an elephant to pay his respects, both that son of brāhmaṇa and Bharima raised this adamantine song (Tib. *rdo-rje'i mgur,* Skt. *vajragīti*) with a loud Brahma voice:

/ gang zhig snying por zhugs pa til gyi mar /
[5a] The sesame oil, which is its essence,
/ rmongs pas til la yod par shes gyur kyang /
Although the ignorant know it is in the sesame seed,
/ rten cing 'brel 'byung yan lag ma shes na /
If they do not know how its constituents are combined,[26]
/ til mar snying po 'byung par mi nus ltar /
They cannot extract the sesame oil, that essence. In the same way
/ lhan cig skyes pa gnyug ma'i ye shes de /
The co-emergent (*sahaja*)[27] innate awareness (*jñāna*),
/ 'gro ba kun gyi snying la yod gyur kyang /
Even if it is present in the hearts of all beings,
/ bla mas ma mtshon rtogs par mi nus so /
Its intuitive knowledge is impossible unless it is pointed out by a guru.
/ til brdungs phub ma bsal bar gyur pa las /
By pounding the sesame and clearing away the husks,
/ til mar snying po byung pa de bzhin du /
One can extract the sesame oil, that essence: similarly,
/ bla ma sten pas de bzhin de nyid don /
When one is close to the guru, the meaning of suchness (tathatā)

/ til mar bzhin du brda' yis bstan par bya /
Will be shown by means of a symbol (*saṅketa*) like the sesame oil.
/ yul rnams dbyer med ngo bo cig tu 'gyur /
The entity of objects is one and inseparable.
/ kye ho ring 'gro gting dpag dka' ba'i don /
O! So far extending, so hard to measure in its depth, the meaning
/ da lta nyid du gsal ba ngo mtshar che /
Is now clear. Wonderful![28]

Thus they sang, and all those who were assembled there were liberated. Unfolding the meaning of the song, "As for the meaning, there is nothing to be rejected even though there is contradiction. There is no antidotal alertness (*gnyen-po ye-shes*)[29] to produce; there is no ground (Tib. *sa*, Skt. *bhūmi*), no path (Tib. *lam*, Skt. *mārga*) to pass, nor is there a fruit (Tib. *'bras-bu*, Skt. *phala*) to attain. The guru must show them simply through conventional symbols (Tib. *kun-rdzob-brda'*, Skt. *saṃvṛti-saṅketa*)!" When he was asked who his guru was, he answered:

/ nga la mi'i bla ma yod /
I have [these] human gurus,
/ klu sgrub tsarya la ba pa /
Nāgārjuna, Cāryapa, Lavapa,
/ skal ba bzang mo bdag gi ni /
Subhaginī,[30] these are my
/ bka' babs bzhi'i bla ma yin /
gurus of the four-fold transmission.[31]

He received the instruction on the illusory body (Tib. *sgyu-lus*, Skt. *māyākāya*) from Nāgārjuna, the dream (Tib. *rmi-lam*, Skt. *svapna*) from Cāryapa, the radiant light (Tib.

'od-gsal, Skt. *prabhāsvara*) from Lavapa, the inner heat (Tib. *gtum-mo,* Skt. *caṇḍālī*) from the Ḍākinī: these are known as the four great rivers of the oral transmission (*snyan-brgyud-kyi chu-bo chen-po bzhi*).[32]

—1.2—

Here is the second [chapter where it is told how] he subdued the Ḍākinīs and asked them to give instruction. Once again the women appeared and spoke:

/ snyan rgyud yi ge med pa ni /
As for the oral transmission beyond words,
/ dri med mkha' 'gro ma la yod /
The stainless Ḍākinīs have it:
/ yid bzhin nor bu rnam gsum long /
You have to obtain this three-fold Wish-Fulfilling Gem![33]

When he said that he would not be able to take it, the women replied with these words:

/ u rgyan gnas kyi ghando lar /
In the temple of fragrance (*gandhālaya*) which is in Uḍḍiyāṇa,
/ lung stan dam tshig ldan pa yis /
One with the prophecy and the commitments (*samaya*)
/ skal ba can gyis blangs na lon /
Of Bhagavatī can take it![34]

When he asked how he could do that, they instructed: [5b] "Take a crystal ladder, a jewel bridge, and a stem of burdock (*rtsa-byi-zung*),[35] then go to Uḍḍiyāṇa!" His father had no difficulty in obtaining those things, so he took them and left.

The Ḍākinī called Jñānaḍākinī of Dharmakāya (*Chos-sku ye-she-kyi mkha'-'gro-ma*) dwelt in the temple of fragrance in the land of Uḍḍiyāṇa, in the West, as a queen. She was in uninterrupted concentration in a sphere beyond duality. Near to her there were the Ḍākinīs called Pañcagotraḍākinīs of Sambhogakāya (*longs-sku rigs-lnga'i mkha'-'gro-ma*). They kept the three-fold Wish-Fulfilling Gem hidden in that jewelled palace. They had locked it with a lock impossible to open, had sealed it with seven seals, and surrounded it with strong walls, a trench, and the castle itself. So they dwelt there as ministers.

Near to them there were the devouring Karma-ḍākinīs of the Nirmāṇakāya (*sprul-sku za-byed las-kyi mkha'-'gro-ma*). They grant spiritual perfection to those who have faith and devotion, but they destroy and devour those who have no faith and whose commitments are imperfect. So they stayed there as guards at the door. That son of brāhmaṇa arrived in the western country of Uḍḍiyāṇa, in front of the temple of fragrance. The Karma-ḍākinīs of the Nirmāṇakāya, with demonic voices or rough, thundering sounds, spoke these words:

/ nga ni sprul sku las kyi mkha' 'gro ma /
We are the Karmaḍākinīs of the Nirmāṇakāya:
/ mi'i sha la dga' zhing khrag la rngams /
We enjoy human flesh and are blood-thirsty![36]

Then they went forth. And that son of brāhmaṇa said:

/ cher 'jigs mkha' 'gro du mas kyang /
Despite many frightening Ḍākinīs,
/ nga'i ba spu'i rtse mi 'gul /
My hairs would not tremble![37]

Thus he said, and his ascetic practice of awareness *(rig-pa-brtul-zhugs)* outshone them. Being firm in body, unopposed in speech and fearless in the mind, he stared at them until they lay senseless. When they recovered from their faint, they spoke:

/ kye ma mar mes sbrang ma rlag pa ltar /
Alas, like the moth is lost at the lamp,
/ khyod zar 'dod pas bdag cag phung /
We wished to eat you, but we have been destroyed.
/ dam pa bdag ni ci dgar mdzod /
Noble one, do whatever you like with us.[38]

At that, the son of brāhmaṇa said: "Let me go inside!" But the Ḍākinīs [6a] replied:

/ bdag cag bran ltar dbang chung pas /
We are like servants, with little power.
/ blon mo dag la ma dris na /
If we do not ask the ministers,
/ bdag cag sha za khrag 'thung mchis /
They will eat our flesh and drink our blood.
/ dam pas nye bar dgongs par mdzod /
Noble one, look upon us with kindness![39]

Then they submitted to the authority of the Ḍākinīs of Sambhogakāya. The latter said: "We will rescue you who have been inferior [to him] in the ascetic practice. So let him come in!" That son of brāhmaṇa put his jewel bridge over the trench, raised his crystal ladder on the wall [and] opened the door with his stem of burdock. Once he was inside, the ministers spoke:

/ 'jigs pa'i sku la 'jigs pa'i gsung /
With frightening bodies and frightening words,

/ 'jigs pa'i mtshon cha thogs nas kyang /
Holding weapons of fear as well,
/ longs sku rigs lnga'i mkha' 'gro ma /
[We are] the Pañcagotraḍākinīs of Sambhogakāya:
/ sha la dga' zhing khrag la rngam /
We enjoy flesh and are blood-thirsty![40]

Thus they spoke, and then the son of brāhmaṇa said:

/ cher 'jigs mkha' 'gro du mas kyang /
Despite many frightening Ḍākinīs,
/ kho bo'i ba spu'i khung mi g.yo /
The roots of my hairs would not waver![41]

Then he stared at them till they lay senseless. "Let me go inside!" he said. But the Ḍākinīs replied:

/ bdag cag blon ltar dbang chung pas /
We are like ministers, with little power.
/ rgyal mo nyid la ma zhus na /
If we do not ask the queen herself,
/ bdag cag bka' chad 'chad pas gcod /
She will punish us.
/ dam pas nye bar dgongs par mdzod /
Noble one, look upon us with kindness![42]

So, after they had supplicated the Dharmakāyaḍākinī, the son [of brāhmaṇa] went in. There was the Jñānaḍākinī of the Dharmakāya and, on her right and left, innumerable heroes (*dpa'-bo*) and heroines (*dpa'-mo*) surrounded her. As that son of brāhmaṇa did not pay homage to her, the assembly said:

/ 'di ni sangs rgyas thams cad kyi /
This [boy, to] the all-Buddhas'
/ yum gyur bcom ldan 'das ma la /
Mother, to Bhagavātī,

/ ma gus tshul can cis mi gzhom /
Does not show respect. Why we do not subdue him?[43]

They were just about to suppress him when the Dharmakāyaḍākinī uttered these words to her retinue:

/ 'di ni sangs rgyas thams cad kyi /
This is the all-Buddhas'
/ yab gyur bde mchog 'khor lo ste /
Father Cakrasaṃvara.
/ mkha' las rdo rje'i char phab kyang /
Even if a rain of vajras fell from the sky,
/ 'di tshe choms par ga la gyur /
How could it subdue him?[44]

[6b] Then the assembly, pretending not to know that man was Cakrasaṃvara, asked him: "Who sent you? Who are you? What do you want?" That son of brāhmaṇa replied:

/ bdag ni paṇ tsa pa na yin /
I am Pañcapana,
/ sring mo bde ster ma yis btang /
My sister Sukhadā sent me.
/ lta spyod 'bras bu dam tshig dang /
The view (*dṛṣṭi*), the action (*caryā*), and the result (*phala*),[45] the commitments, and
/ sku gsum nor bu leṅ du yongs /
The Wish-Fulfilling Gem of the three Bodies: I came here to receive them.[46]

Those in the assembly uttered an embarrassing laugh, making fun of him, and spoke in one voice:

/ dmus long bltas pas gzugs mi mthong /
A born-blind looks at, but he cannot see the forms;

/ 'on pas nyan pas sgra mi thos /
A deaf man listens to, but he cannot hear the sounds;
/ lkugs pas smras pas don mi go /
An idiot speaks, but he cannot understand the meaning.
/ bdud kyis bslus la bden pa med /
No truth is there in those deceived by Māra![47]

The master replied to them:

/ nyes pa zad pa rdzun gyi tshig /
[When] evil is consumed, false words
/ smra bar mi 'gyur rgyu med phyir /
Are not spoken: there would be no cause.
/ bdud min mkha' 'gro ma ru bden /
No matter of Māra: in a Ḍākinī is the truth![48]

Then the Jñānaḍākinī caused these [three] signs to appear: the drawing of a sacred image (*tsa-ka-li*) for the Body, a script for the Speech and some sacred attributes (*phyag-mtshan*) for the Mind.[49] That son of brāhmaṇa spoke:

/ snang stong sku'i gsang mdzod nas /
From the secret treasure of the Body where appearance and nothingness coalesce (pratibhāsa-śūnya),[50]
/ mthun mongs yid bzhin nor bu zhu /
I beg the Wish-Fulfilling Gem, the common one.
/ brjod bral gsung gi gsang mdzod nas /
From the secret treasure of the Word which is beyond any expression,
/ dam tshig yid bzhin nor bu zhu /
I beg the Wish-Fulfilling Gem, the commitments one.
/ rtog med thugs kyi gsang mdzod nas /
From the secret treasure of the Mind which is beyond cognition,

/ gnas lugs yid bzhin nor bu zhu /
I beg the Wish-Fulfilling Gem, the reality one.[51]

At that, Jñānaḍākinī spoke:

/ thun mongs yid bzhin nor bu la /
As for the common Wish-Fulfilling Gem,
/ lung bstan nyams kyi lde mig dgos /
One needs the key of what has been expressed through the prophecy:
/ lung ma bstan pas phyed mi 'gyur /
Who did not get such a prophecy cannot open.
/ dam tshig yid bzhin nor bu la /
As for the commitments' Wish-Fulfilling Gem,
/ bka' rgyud zab mo'i lde mig dgos /
One needs the key of the profound oral transmission:
/ gnyen po med pas phyed mi 'gyur /
Who has not the antidotes cannot open.
/ gnas lugs yid bzhin nor bu la /
As for the reality Wish-Fulfilling Gem,
/ shes rab zab mo'i lde mig dgos /
One needs the key of the profound discriminating awareness (*prajñā*):[52]
/ rtogs pa med pas phyed mi 'gyur /
Who has no cognition cannot open.[53]

Thus she spoke, and that son of brāhmaṇa replied:

/ mkha' 'gro'i gsang tshig thugs kyi sdom /
The secret word of the Ḍākinī is the Mind pledge (*samvara*);
/ ma rig mun sel ye shes sgron /
What dispels the darkness of nescience (*avidyā*) is the light of transcending awareness (*jñāna*);

/ rang rig rang byung rang gsal gyi /
Self-awareness (*svasaṃvitti, svasaṃvedanā*) is self-originated (*svayambhū*) and self-irradiating.
/ lung bstan nyams kyi lde mig yod /
I have the key of what has been expressed through the prophecy.
/ gang yang skye ba med pa yi /
When nothing [7a] is conceived any longer,
/ sems nyid rang grol chos sku la /
It is the being as such of thinking (*cittatā*), the Dharmakāya of self-liberation:
/ rang grol phyag rgya chen por shar /
This self-liberation arises in the Great Seal (*mahāmudrā*).[54]
/ dam tshig rang grol lde mig yod /
I have the key of the self-liberation of commitments.
/ dmigs pa yid la mi byed cing /
A mind where there is no mental elaboration (*amanasikāra*),
/ dran pa rdul tsam ma skyes pa'i /
Where even a particle of dust of recollection (*smṛti*) will not arise,
/ sems nyid chos nyid chos sku la /
This is the being as such of thinking, the Dharmakāya of the being of phenomena (*dharmatā*).
/ mthong pa nyams kyi lde mig yod /
I have the key to enter the vision.[55]

Thus he spoke, and both the Sambhoga and the Nirmāṇakāya of the Jñānaḍākinī in one voice joined to raise this song:

/ bdag cag yab gcig bcom ldan 'das /
You are our father, you are Bhagavān!

/ te lo sangs rgyas 'gro ba'i mgon /
You are Tilopa Buddha, you are the Protector of beings!
/ 'khor lo bde mchog bde ba che /
You are Cakrasaṃvara, the Great Bliss!
/ yid bzhin nor bu rnam gsum 'bul /
We offer you the three-fold Wish-Fulfilling Gem![56]

After that, they explained the 51st chapter of the root tantra [of Cakrasaṃvara][57] and then, together with the tantra, they gave him the oral transmission.

Then Jñānaḍakinī spoke: "If you want to attain my Body, be assiduous in the Developing Stage; [as to my] Word, [be assiduous in] the heart; [as to my] Mind, be assiduous in the Great Seal of the Fulfilment Stage. Go to the monastery of Śiromaṇi (*gTsug-gi nor-bu*) and take care of the three, Nāropa, Riripa and Kasoripa!" Then the noblest of ladies disappeared. He was given the name Tilopa Prajñābhadra. He spoke:

/ kho bos mkha' la bya bzhin du /
I, like a bird in the sky,
/ 'od gsal sems kyi bya 'phur nas /
A bird of clear light thinking which is flying away,
/ thog med shes rab bzang po 'gro /
Without obstacles, Prajñābhadra is going![58]

And the Ḍākinīs of both Sambhoga and Nirmāṇakāya spoke:

/ dam pa khyod ni ji lta bu /
You, noble one, why so?
/ bdag cag don du bzhugs par zhu /
We beg you to remain for our benefit.[59]

Thus they begged, and Tilopa replied:

/ gtso mo nyid kyi lung bstan ltar /
As the noblest of ladies herself prophesied,
/ snod ldan don du rnal 'byor bdag /
For the benefit of fitting vessels, as a yogin, I
/ gtsug gi nor bu'i dgon par 'gro /
Am going to the monastery of Śiromaṇi.[60]

After that, while he was on his way, he received a nine-fold Dharma of the formless Ḍākinīs from the air element of space:[61]

/ lus med mkha' 'gro'i rdo rje'i gsung /
These are adamantine words of the formless Ḍākinis:
/ dri za'i glu dbyangs snyan pa ltar /
Like a melody of the Gandharvas, a heavenly song,
/ bar snang stong las 'di ltar thos /
They are heard from the void space!

/ smin grol sems kyi rgya mdud bshig /
The ripening and liberation is to loosen the knots of thinking.
/ dam tshig rang sems me long ltos /
The commitments are to examine the mirror of one's thinking activity.
/ rtsa rlung gra mig 'khor lo bskor /
[7b] Circumambulate the wheels (*cakra*) of the [coiling] energy channels (*nāḍī*) and winds (*vāyu*) [through their] eyelets.
/ bde chen gsung gi rin chen zung /
The Great Bliss is to hold the jewel of the Word.
/ rig pa ye shes sgron me ltos /
The intrinsic awareness (*vidyā*) is to look at the torch of transcending awareness (*jñāna*).
/ rang grol phyag rgya chen po ltos /
The self-liberation is to look at the Great Seal.

/ dam rdzas rtogs pa'i nyi ma lde /
The substance of commitments is to be warmed by the sun of a clear cognition.
/ spyod pa chu la ral gri rgyob /
The action is to strike the water with a sword.
/ ro snyoms phyi'i me long ltos /
The sameness of taste (*samarasa*) is in looking at the outer mirror.[62]

Having listened to these [words] from space, Tilopa then spoke:

/ gtso mo ji lta'i tshul ston te /
O noblest of ladies! such a way having been shown,
/ sgyu ma lus kyi ghan do lar /
In the temple of the illusory body
/ lus med mkha' 'gro'i gsang bcug nas /
Having put the secret of the formless Ḍākinīs,
/ brjod med ngag gis lcags bcug ste /
With a word beyond expression, I will put a seal on it.
/ 'od gsal sems kyi bya 'phur 'gro /
The bird of radiating thinking would fly away![63]

Then he went to the temple of the monastery of Śiromaṇi.

—1.3—

Here is the third [chapter where it is told how] he had no human gurus. Many people came to him; they attained perfections and obtained the teaching [he had received] from the temple of fragrance. When he was asked who his guru was, he answered:

/ nga la mi'i bla ma med /
I have no human guru.

/ bla ma thams cad mkhyen pa yin /
My guru is the Omniscient One (Sarvajña)![64]

—1.4—

As to the fourth [chapter where it is told how] he showed himself in various ways, there are eight [episodes]: first, he outshone a yogin, then he subdued a heretic, a magician, a barmaid, a singer, a butcher, one who denied the law of cause and effect, and a powerful sorcerer.[65]

—1.4.1—

Here is the first [episode].[66] In South India there was a king who loved his mother dearly. He would do anything to please her. He asked his mother what her preference was with respect to root virtues. When he invited her to propose a virtuous act which he would then perform, his mother said: "Gather paṇḍitas, siddhas and Ḍākinīs. Then, once a jewelled maṇḍala is raised in the sky, if you have the empowerments and a gaṇacakra performed, I would be happy."

So he did this: he sent a messenger to every paṇḍita and siddha to invite them. The paṇḍitas performed the purification of the place and so forth, and the others declared that everything was carried out correctly. But a woman bearing the signs of ugliness came before those sages (*ku-sa-li*)[67] and asked: "Who will lead [8a] this gaṇacakra?" 'Dran-za-med-pa (the "Unequalled-one") said: "I will do it." She replied: "You cannot do it! My brother will come and lead it." "Where is he?" he asked. "He lives in a cemetery," she answered. "In that case, fetch him!" he ordered. "I will go and fetch him. Wait here for his coming!" she said. Later they arrived. Then 'Dran-za-med-pa and the other (Tilopa) sat on two thrones.

They were a match for each other in the topics of valid cognition (Tib. *tshad-ma*, Skt. *pramāṇa*). Again, when [both] drew a maṇḍala in the sky that would fade neither in rain nor wind, they matched each other. Then, when [both,] riding on lions, had the sun and moon running a race, [once again] they were evenly matched. However, Tilopa made the sun and moon fall down on the ground, and rode over them on a lion. Then he turned himself inside out and manifested a maṇḍala with a cemetery for every single hair [of his]; he manifested a tree in each of them and, on every tree, he was sitting cross-legged, in a playful mood, and so forth. As 'Dran-zla-med-pa was not able to match this, he said, "That is wonderful! Where does such a miracle come from?"

/ ngo mtshar spyod pa ci las byung /
Where does this man causing wonder come from?

[Tilopa] answered with a song:

/ kye ma 'dug na nam kha'i dkyil du 'dug /
Oh! If sitting, sit in the sky.
/ nyal na mdung gi rtse la nyal /
If sleeping, sleep on the top of a spear.
/ lta na nyi zla'i dkyil du ltos /
If looking, look into the sun and the moon.
/ don dam rtogs pa'i te lo pa /
Having realized the ultimate truth (paramārtha), Tilopa
/ nga ni 'bad rtsol kun dang bral /
Am I! the one beyond any efforts!

Thus he sang and, as he spoke on the inconceivable presence of the given (Tib. *rang-bzhin*, Skt. *svabhāva*), all were liberated. ['Dran-zla-med-pa] was then named Nus-ldan Blo-gros. And he continues to live in Uḍḍiyāṇa in a deathless state.

—1.4.2—

Here is the second [paragraph where it is told how] he subdued the heretic.[68] In Śrī-Nālanda there was a siddha of heretical doctrine. All the Buddhists and non-Buddhists had to rise in his presence; if they didn't, they had to engage in a contest with him either in debate or in magical powers.

Once, when Tilopa did not rise, he said, "So you are keen to debate and exercise your magical powers: [8b] let us contest!" After that, all the Buddhist and non-Buddhist paṇḍitas gathered there with the king sitting in the middle. The doctrine of the winner would be accepted: they therefore debated and the heretic was defeated. Even in the competition of powers Tilopa was unmatched. The heretic, shooting flames from his mouth [towards him], asked:

/ khams gsum kun kyang g.yo byed pa'i /
[I am] the shaker of all the three realms;
/ nga yis mi 'jigs su zhig yin /
Who are you whom I have not terrified?

Once [Tilopa] had deflected [the flames], he answered in a song:

/ blta na dmus long mig gis ltos /
When looking, look with blind eyes.
/ skom na smig rgyu'i chu la 'thung /
If thirsty, drink the water of a mirage.
/ bying na bum pa rlung gis khengs /
When sinking down, fill up the vase with winds.[69]
/ 'jigs pa kun bral te lo yin /
Beyond any fear, I am Tilopa.

Thus he sang and, as he spoke on the inconceivable being of phenomena, all were liberated. [The heretic] was then named Nag-po dGe-ba. And he continues to live in Sil-ba'i Tshal in a deathless state.

—1.4.3—

Here is the third [paragraph where it is told how] he subdued the magician.[70] There was a king threatened with expulsion from the country by a magician with a magic army. A woman bearing the signs of ugliness came there: "Who will command your army?" she asked the people. When they answered that such a one would do it, the woman replied, "That one will not [be able to] do it. My brother will!" "Where is your brother?" they asked. She said: "One yojana (*dpag-tshad*) far [from here,] in a cemetery, there is an Aloes tree. [My brother] has fixed the tail of a horse on it; then, he has tied the legs and the hands of a corpse to that [tail]: he is there, hanging on that [corpse] and swinging."

When the king was informed, he said: "That woman related three impossible messages: bring her here!" But, when she was interrogated, she repeated what she had said before. He sent [someone] to check, and things were just as she had described. Tilopa was invited [before the king]. As [the army] did not know it was [just] magic, they were about to flee, but [Tilopa] destroyed that magic [army], killed all [the illusory soldiers] and caught the magician. After that, the magician spoke:

/ chos la rten pa'i skyes bu khyod /
One who relies on the Dharma, you!
/ de ltar bsod pa mngag ma rigs /
It is not right to kill in this way!

[9a] [Tilopa] answered with a song:

/ sgyu ma'i dmag tshogs bsad pa la /
Killing magic soldiers
/ sems med phyir na sdig pa med /
Is no sin, because they are not living beings!
/ bsod na sgyu ma'i skyes bu bsod /
When killing, I kill illusory creatures.
/ sgom na dbugs bral lta bur bsgoms /
When meditating, I meditate beyond respiration.
/ smra na lkugs pa'i lce yis smros /
When speaking, speak with a dumb tongue.
/ 'dod na yi ge zad par skyol /
When affirming, employ all the letters.

Thus he sang and, when he spoke on the inconceivable substance of what is existent (Tib. *dngos-po*, Skt. *vastu*, *bhāva*), all were liberated. [The magician] was then named Slu-byed bDen-smra. And he continues to live in Ha-ha sGrog-pa in a deathless state.

—1.4.4—

Here is the fourth [paragraph where it is told how] he subdued the barmaid.[71] She was selling her beer when a monkey and a cat which were emanated by Tilopa sucked and drank the beer. She burst into tears. People asked her what had happened, and she told the story. "Ask that yogin!" people said. Weeping, the barmaid said:

/ bdag gi 'tsho ba chad pas na /
Since I am deprived of my livelihood,
/ thugs rje rjes su bzung du gsol /
I beg you to look graciously [upon me].

In a moment, all the jugs were again filled with beer. Then [Tilopa] sang a song:

/ skom na dug chu khol ma 'thung /
If thirsty, drink poisonous boiled water.
/ 'phro na spre'u ded la sod /
When it has been emanated, chase and kill the monkey.
/ gnyen po sgom chen byi la rten (bsten) /
The antidote is to hold the cat of the great meditation.
/ thams cad lhan skyes ro ru bsgyur /
Everything will take the taste of the simultaneously-arisen.
/ don dam sprang po te lo pa /
Tilopa, the beggar of the ultimate truth,
/ khyod kyis mthong med rnal 'byor yin /
A yogin am I, and you did not see!

Thus he sang and, when he spoke on the inconceivable Great Bliss, all were liberated. [The barmaid] was then named Nyi-'od sGron-ma. And she continues to live in So-sa-gling in a deathless state.

—1.4.5—

Here is the fifth [paragraph where it is told how] he subdued the singer.[72] There was a skilful singer. Tilopa sang a song before him. "I challenge you," he said, so they went into competition. "Sing a song, then it will be my turn," the master said.

When [the singer] had finished his songs, the master sang unceasingly. [9b] The other had not been able to do the same, so he said:

/ nga ni tshangs pa'i 'jig rten yang /
As for me, even the world of Brahma

/ skyeng par byed pa'i glu mkhan yin /
I can embarrass as a singer!

[Tilopa] answered with a song:

/ skyo na dri za'i grong khyer ltos /
If sad, look at the city of Gandharvas,
/ nyan na bung ba'i glu la nyon /
When listening, listen to the song of the bees,
/ lta na dmus long mig gis ltos /
When looking, look with blind eyes,
/ thos yul rnams ni brag cha 'dra /
The sounds you perceive are just like echoes.

Thus he sang and, when he spoke on the inconceivable music, all were liberated. [The singer] was then named Byangs-ldan lKugs-pa. And he continues to live in Na-ga-ra in a deathless state.

—1.4.6—

Here is the sixth [paragraph where it is told how] he subdued the butcher.[73] This butcher used to kill all animals' offspring to nourish his son. [Once,] he took the lid off the cooking pot in order to boil some meat and give it to his son, but Tilopa had transformed it into the arms and legs of the boy. He said:

/ rang gis byas pa'i sdig pa de /
[Is] that bad action of mine
/ rang la 'khor ram ji ltar yin /
Coming back to me? How is that?

He was tormented by affliction. "So then!" [Tilopa] said to him. "If you do not kill any longer, your son will be restored." As he had promised, [Tilopa] uttered in a song:

/ 'byed na mar khu dangs snyigs 'byed /
When separating, one separates the clear fluid from the sediments.
/ sreg na dus mtha' me yis sregs /
When cooking, one cooks with an endless fire.
/ 'don na rlung sems spyi bor thon /
When ejecting, one has to eject the vital principle of consciousness through the crown of the head.[74]
/ 'khrud na sems kyi dri ma khrus /
When washing, one washes the defilements in one's thinking activity.

Thus he sang and, when he spoke on the inconceivable killing, all were liberated. [The butcher] was then named bDe-byed dGa'-ba. And he continues to live in Srin-po'i Gling in a deathless state.

—1.4.7—

Here is the seventh [paragraph where it is told how] he subdued the one who denied the [law of] cause and effect (Tib. *rgyu-'bras,* Skt. *hetu-phala*).[75] A Materialist (Tib. *rgyang-phan-pa,* Skt. *lokāyata*)[76] who used to speak against the [law of] cause and effect declared that there is no karma, no virtue, no sin. A Buddhist said that, according to the Buddha, there are these things. They appointed the master [Tilopa] as judge of the debate. The master de-clared that the one affirming the reality of karma, [that is of the law of] cause and effect had won. But the Materia-list said: "I cannot see it properly."

[10a] So the master took him and manifested the heavens and the hells to him. In a heavenly residence there was a goddess who was alone. When [the Materialist] asked why, he was told that she was the consort of a virtuous heretic she was helping [in changing his view].

Then [Tilopa] took him and they went to the hells: [many] copper pots were there and, in each of them, a human being. But one of them was empty. When [the Materialist] asked what was cooking there, [Tilopa] answered that all heretics denying karma and [the law of] cause and effect were cooked there. He was alarmed and said:

/ las kyis bsags pa'i sdig pa yi /
Sins accumulated by karma
/ dmyal ba rang gi sems la 'khor /
Come back in one's own mind as hell;
/ las kyis bsags pa'i dge ba yis /
Virtues accumulated by karma
/ mtho ris rang gi sems la 'khor /
Come back in one's own mind as heaven.

[Tilopa] answered with a song:

/ chags na dur khrod gling du skyol /
If attached, go to a cemetery.
/ rgud na rgyal mtshan rtse la phyogs /
If in trouble, raise the banner.
/ rnam par rtog pa sprul sku ste /
A clear notion (*vikalpa*) is the Nirmāṇakāya.
/ ngas ni bstan pa ci yang med /
Actually, I did not show anything [to you].

Thus he sang and, when he spoke on the inconceivable variety and multiplicity (*sna-tshogs*), all were liberated. [The Materialist] was then named Dzi-na Byang-chub. He continues to live on Śrīparvata (*dPal-gyi ri*) in a deathless state.

He [Tilopa] took other bodily manifestations and explained the Dharma to sinners. He showed himself in innumerable ways: as an artisan, as a great meditating siddha, as a fisherman, as a hunter, and so forth. Those [sinners] said:

/ nya pa la sogs pa byed pa /
[You are the] one who works as a fisherman, and so on...

And, when [Tilopa] replied,

/ don dam rtogs pa'i te lo pa /
Tilopa, the one who has the clear notion of the ultimate truth,
/ dge sdig zhes bya'i ming yang med /
There is no name for what is called virtue or sin!

they asked for instruction.

—1.4.8—

Here is the eighth [paragraph where it is told how] he subdued the powerful sorcerer (*mthu-mkhan*).[77] There was a powerful sorcerer who used to bewitch people and cause their deaths. When Tilopa saw that the right time for subduing him had come, the two entered into a competition of killing.

Tilopa brought back from death those who had died while in contest with each other, but he did not restore to life some women and others [of the sorcerer's retinue. He looked at him and] thought, "He also looks like an old tree trunk!" Then he said, "Now, if I return your people to life, will you cease to bewitch [others]?" The [sorcerer], not [yet] recovered, said:

/ sos pa med pa'i spyod pa 'di /
This action for which there is no recovery,
/ shan pa rang dang khyad med dam /
Isn't it just like that of the butcher?

[Tilopa] answered in a song:

/ ltos cig rang gi sems la bltos /
Look! You have to look into your own thinking (*svacitta*):
/ snang ba'i ri bo khyur mid kyis /
By swallowing the mountain of appearance,
/ rgya mtsho chen po hub kyis thob /
By drinking the great ocean in one draught, you will get it.
/ 'khor ba'i ltos thag chod la zhog /
Saṃsāra bonds are to be severed.

Thus he sang and, when he spoke on the inconceivable virtuous activities (*'phrin-las*), all were liberated. [The powerful sorcerer] was then named Nyi-i-mi. And he continues to live in Ki-mi-tsi-ki-li.

—2—

Here is the second [section where it is told how] he appeared as a manifestation of Cakrasaṃvara.[78] In East India, near Nadukata, on the bank of the Khasu river [next to] the cemetery of rMa-sha'i Tshal, there is the Aśoka monastery where Tilopa's uncle and mother—[the latter was, at that time,] a nun—were abbot (*upādhyāya*) and teacher (*ācārya*). [Tilopa] embraced the religious life, and was named bikṣu (*dge-long*) Kalapa. The other [monks] were engaged in the three wheels (*'khor-gsum*)[79] but he, instead of undergoing the spiritual trainings (*chos-spyod*),[80] would kill lots of locusts, piling up their heads on one side and their bodies on the other.

All [the monks] became involved in blaming him for that, in particular the monk who was in charge of discipline, who said: "We will have a conference, gathering all those who are in the Dharma, particularly the monks, and most particularly the monks of the [monastery of] Aśoka." So they did, and the king of that country spoke [to him]:

/ btsun gzugs srog chags bsad pa khyod /
[How is that] you, apparently a monk, kill insects?
/ yul dang mkhan slob su zhig yin /
Where is your place, who are your abbot and teacher?

[Tilopa] answered in a song:

/ dgon pa mya ngan med pa yin /
The monastery is Aśoka.
/ mkhan slob ma dang zhang po yin /
Uncle and mother are abbot and teacher.
/ bdag rang dge slong te lo yin /
I am the bikṣu Tilopa.
/ nga yis skal pa bye ba ru /
Millions of kalpas ago, I
/ zhing khams brgya ru nga yis phyin /
Went to a hundred [Buddha]fields.
/ klu sgrub ārya de wa dang /
Nāgārjuna, Āryadeva, and
/ sangs rgyas rnams dang nga gtam byas /
The Buddhas: with them did I speak!
/ ngas ni sangs rgyas stong yang mthong /
I saw the thousand Buddhas as well.
/ ngas ni sems can bsad pa med /
I have not killed any sentient being!

Thus having sung, it was said that the locusts began to buzz and flew away. [At that] all believed, and then he was celebrated as a manifestation of Cakrasaṃvara.

—3—

Here is the third [section where] he is asserted to be Cakrasaṃvara himself.[81] A king of a country, in East India, invited all those who arrived there to beg for alms. They were venerated by the people because, while going out [for alms], they would step in a decent way, their eyes never looking at a distance greater than one yoke, and would recite verses agreeable to hear; while coming back, they would pronounce words of blessing for what had been given [to them]. When they paid him respect, the king said [to them]: "For what has been given, everyone [of you] has to recite verses of blessing not in contradiction with the words of the grammarians, nor with the arguments of valid cognition, the scriptural tradition (Tib. *lung,* Skt.*āgama*), the oral instructions (Tib. *man-ngag,* Skt. *upadeśa*), the experiences, and the realizations of those having a clear realization (*rtog-pa-can-rnams-kyi rtogs-pa*)." So all recited [verses], one by one, without contradiction and in harmony with [those of] the other. When it was the turn of the master, [the verses] he recited were [simultaneously] in harmony with all [the others]. When he had finished, the king asked [him] about those [verses] and their meaning.

/ bdag la pha ma ma mchis te /
I have neither father nor mother:
/ 'khor lo bde mchog bde ba'i mchog /
[I am] Cakrasaṃvara, the sublime Bliss.
/ bdag la mkhan slob ma mchis te /
I have neither abbot nor teacher:
/ bdag ni rang byung sangs rgyas yin /
I am the self-born Buddha.
/ bdag la sgra tshad ma mchis te /
I have neither grammar nor arguments of valid cognition:

/ gtan tshigs rig pa rang brdol yin /
The science of logic (Tib. *gtan-tshigs-rig-pa,* Skt. *hetu-vidyā*)[82] came up by itself.
/ bde mchog sku gsung thugs dang ni /
As to the Body, Speech and Mind of Cakrasaṃvara,
/ lus ngag yid gsum dbyer ru med /
They are one with [my] body, speech and mind.
/ nga ni bde ba chen por 'gro /
I go into the Great Bliss!

Thus having sung, he was celebrated as Cakrasaṃvara himself.

—4—

Here is the fourth [section where it is told how] he appeared as the synthesis of the bodies of all the Buddhas of the three times.[83] The king Siṃhacandra (*Seng-ge-zla-ba*) invited many siddhas. When he had made offerings [to them], he asked [them] to give the empowerment. In response, Tilopa caused a maṇḍala of coloured powder to appear in space. As he was perceived in different ways [by the others], Tilopa uttered in a song:

/ bdag lus kye kye'i rdo rje la /
I am Hevajra in the body,
/ ngag ni ma hā ma ya yin /
Mahāmāyā in the speech,
/ sems ni bde mchog 'khor lo ste /
Cakrasaṃvara in the mind,
/ phung khams gsang ba 'dus pa la /
Guhyasamāja in the aggregates (*skandha*) and elements (*dhātu*),
/ yan lag nag po sgra rgyud nyid /
Kṛṣṇayamāri in the limbs,

/ nying lag rdo rje 'jigs byed la /
Vajrabhairava in the subtler parts of the body,
/ ba spu dus gsum sangs rgyas yin /
The Buddhas of the three times in the hairs.

Thus having sung, Tilopa was celebrated as the synthesis of the Bodies of all the Buddhas.

When the deeds of such a man were at their end, the living beings of Za-hor in East India led to spiritual ripening and liberation [were so many that] seven towns of one hundred thousand [inhabitants each] were emptied.

After that, [how] he had attained the siddhis, and was also celebrated as a Nirmāṇakāya, the account of the lord of yoga Tilopa—[that is] the text of his great qualities, of the deeds performed by him—[such a text] had been composed separately but in a complete form. [Now,] in the monastery of Gro-bo-lung, I have composed it for [my] son mDo-sde.

Maṅgalaṃ!

Notes

NOTES TO PREFACE

1. Fol. 2a.3: *mDo sde'i don phyir yi ger bkod pa;* fol. 11b.3: *sras mDo sde'i don du yi ger bkod pa.*
2. Other hagiographies of Tilopa are available in photostat reproduction. But they have been less useful to us because either they were written too recently to be considered consistent as sources, or they gave help in checking neither the biographical events nor the poetical passages in our text. For example, there is also a very short *Ti-lo dang Nā-ro'i rnam-thar* by sGam-po-pa bSod-nams-rin-chen (1079-1153), in *gSung-'bum,* vol. *ka—bSod-nams-rin-chen-gyi rnam-thar-rgyan,* fols. 1a-8b; but the text, even if very ancient and by such an author, is not an actual account of Tilopa's life, as it mostly concerns Nāropa.
3. English "Foreword" (p. 2) to the photostat reproduction of the text.
4. *Phyag-rgya chen-po bsam-gyis-mi-khyab-pa,* vol. *pu* fol. 139b.1 of the sNar-thang edition of *bsTan-'gyur,* vol. *pu* fol. 145a.4 of the Peking edition (Cordier, vol. LXXIII, no. 32; *TT,* vol. LXXXII, no. 4635, p. 38), vol. *zhi* fol. 245b.3 of the sDe-dge edition (*Tôhoku,* nos. 2305-2312), and vol. *zhi* fol. 245b.3 of the Co-ne edition.
5. *Phyag-rgya chen-po'i man-ngag,* vol. *tsi* fol. 144a.4 of the sNar-thang, vol. *tsi* fol. 155b.8 of the Peking (Cordier, vol. XLVII, no. 26; *TT,* vol. LXIX, no. 3132, p. 134), vol. *zhi* fol. 242b.7 of the sDe-dge (*Tôhoku,* no. 2303), and vol. *zhi* fol. 242b.7 of the Co-ne edition of the *bsTan-'gyur.*

NOTES TO TRANSLITERATION OF TIBETAN TEXT

1. *rgyas-gdab*: *gdab,* written in *dbu-can,* has been added below the line.

2. *bya'o*: the letter *'a*, written in *dbu-can*, has been added below the line, while its *na-ro is* above it.
3. *sgra-khcan*: the letter *kha* has been written below the line.
4. *don phyir*: a syllable has been written between *don* and *phyir*, and then deleted.
5. *bla-ma-med-par*: the syllable *ma* has been written in *dbu-can* in place of another one which has been deleted.
6. *bhe-ha-ra*: the syllable *ha*, written in *dbu-can*, has been added below the line with a mark to show where it should be inserted.
7. *srang-mdo*: the syllable *srang*, written in *dbu-can*, has been added below the line.
8. *brgya-stong-pa ci-yang mi-nyes*: *brgya-stong-pa* and *nyes*, written in *dbu-can*, have been added below the line.
9. *bang-ga-la'i*: the syllable *ga*, written in *dbu-can*, has been added below the line.
10. *byas-pas rgya-gar-skad-du*: *byas* and *skad*, written in *dbu-can*, have been added below the line.
11. *pas*: the letter *sa*, written in *dbu-can*, has been added below the line.
12. *dka'-ba'i don*: the syllable *ba'i*, written in *dbu-can*, has been added below the line.
13. There is a long blank space between *rgyal* and *mo*.
14. *za-byed*, written in *dbu-can*, has been added below the line.
15. *rgyal-bar gyur-to*: the syllable *rgyal*, written in *dbu-can*, has been added below the line.
16. *du-mas*: the syllable *du*, written in *dbu-can*, has been written below the line.
17. *'chad*: the letter *'a* has been added below the line.
18. *gsungs*: the second *sa*, written in *dbu-can*, has been added below the line.
19. This verse and the following one have been added in *dbu-can* script at the bottom of the page, with a mark at the line where they are to be inserted.
20. *gsungs*: the second *sa*, written in *dbu-can*, has been added below the line.

21. Something has been deleted between *tu* and *mgur*.
22. *'dran-zla-med-pa*: the syllable *zla*, written in *dbu-can*, has been added above the line.
23. *ma-byung*, written in *dbu-can*, has been added above the line.
24. *de-la mi-ro'i rkang-pa rtag / de'i lag-pa-la yang rta-lnga rtag-ste*: these two sentences have been added in *dbu-can* at the bottom of the page, with a mark at the line where they are to be inserted.
25. *sgyu-ma'i*: the syllable *ma'i*, written in *dbu-can*, has been added above the line.
26. *lce-yis*: the letter *sa* has been added in *dbu-can* below the line.
27. *lo-rgyus*: the syllable *rgyus*, written in *dbu-can* below the line, is apparently in place of the wrong short form *lo(-rgyu)s, which should have a zhabs-kyu*; the letter *sa*, for *(rgyu)s*, has not been deleted.
28. A syllable has been deleted between *na* and *gzhan*.
29. *rlung-sems*: the syllable *sems*, written in *dbu-can* above the line, is apparently in place of the wrong short form *rlung (-sems)* which should have a *'greng-bu*; the letter *sa*, for *(sem)s*, has not been deleted.
30. *'dor*: the letter *'a* has been added below the line.
31. *slob-ma*: the syllable *ma* has been added below the line.
32. *smin-grol-la*: the particle *la* has been added in *dbu-can* below the line.
33. *dbang-phyug*: the syllable *phyug*, written in *dbu-can*, has been added below the line.

NOTES TO TRANSLATION OF TIBETAN TEXT

1. The nine features of dance (*gar dgu'i nyams*) are: charming, heroic, ugly, aggressive, smiling, wrathful, compassionate, frightening, and peaceful (*TEDBT*, s.v. *gar-gyi nyams dgu*). The phrase *spros-bral mkha'-khyab gar dgu'i nyams* seems to allude in a metaphorical way to the three Buddhakāyas: *dharmakāya* (*chos-kyi sku*), *sambhogakāya* (*longs-spyod-rdzogs-pa'i*

sku), and *nirmāṇakāya* (*sprul-pa'i sku*). As for the Sanskrit word *kāya*, it is useful to mention what H. Guenther has so often pointed out, that we have here a name for a dynamic process: a 'structure of experience' (Guenther 1968: 215-216), not a 'thing'. In this perspective, since Tibetan language is more analytic as to meaning than Sanskrit (Guenther 1959-60: 84), it distinguishes between *lus*, that is the mere 'organismic being' (Guenther 1963/1: 135-136), and *sku*—here translated as "Body"—which "expresses the idea of existence in an almost Parmenidian sense" (Guenther 1966: 143-144).

2. Prajñābhadra is one of the names of Tilopa; rDo-rje-mdzes-'od (fol. 43b.2) informs us that the other ones are Mahāsukhavajra (*bDe-chen-rdo-rje*), Nirvikalpavajra (*rTog-med-rdo-rje*), Sukhacakra (*bDe-ba'i 'khor-lo*) and Kālapa (*Ka-la-pa*).
3. *byin-gyis brlobs*. The term *byin-brlabs* is for Skt.*adiṣṭhāna*, which means 'basis' or 'support'. As such, the spiritual "basis" for successful practice is the grace or blessing of the *guru* or, as in this case, of the *ḍākinī*.
4. The Tibetan translation of the Sanskrit Cakrasaṃvara can be bDe-mchog, 'Khor-lo-sdom-pa, or their contraction bDe-mchog-'Khor-lo. These names call to mind the yoga experience of 'bliss' (*bde*), the 'supreme one' (*mchog*). Such an experience comes into existence when the focal points (*'khor-lo*) of the subtle body are reintegrated into a dynamic synthesis (*sdom-pa*) (Guenther 1963/2: 4).
5. This distinction between *neyārtha* and *nītārtha* which is so common in Buddhist texts "roughly corresponds to the various degrees of the student's intellectual acumen" (Guenther 1958: 61).
6. Jago (Tib. *Dza-go, Dza-ko, Dzā-ko*, or *'Jha-go*) is far from any definite geographical location. According to Tāranātha (*bKa'-babs bdun-ldan*: 45) Tilopa would have been from Caṭighābo, or Caṭigharo, which, as has been suggested by A. Chattopadhyaya (*rGya-gar chos-'byung*: 255), could be identified with the modern Chittagong. We do not reach any stronger certainty in locating the Bengali principality of Sahor (Tib.

Za-hor), where Atīśa was also from. Apart from taking the word *sahor* (or *śahor*) as a common Indian name of Persian origin for "city" (Chatterji 1926: I, 192 ff.; Chattopadhyaya 1967: 62), it has been observed by S.K. De (1943: I, 33) that "this place Za-hor is conjectured in turns to be Lahore and Jessore in South Bengal (Waddel and Sarat Chandra Das) and Sabhar in East Bengal (H.P. Sastri) [...]. A.H. Francke would probably identify it with Mandi in North-Western India...". G. Roerich (*Deb-ther sngon-po*: 241), like Shastri, would identify it with Sabhar, presently in Dacca district.

7. Cf. O-rgyan-pa: 7a.4; rDo-rje-mdzes-'od: 27b.5; Mon-rtse-pa: 12b.3; gTsang-smyon He-ru-ka: 9b.5; Kun-dga'-rin-chen: 11b.5; dBang-phyug-rgyal-mtshan: 7b.2; lHa-btsun: 5b.2.
8. Cf. rGyal-thang-pa: 5b.3; O-rgyan-pa: 7b.1; rDo-rje-mdzes-'od: 27b.6; Mon-rtse-pa: 12b.7; gTsang-smyon He-ru-ka: 10a.2; Kun-dga'-rin-chen: 11b.6; dBang-phyug-rgyal-mtshan: 8b.4; lHa-btsun: 6a.3.
9. Cf. rGyal-thang-pa: 5b.4; O-rgyan-pa: 7b2; rDo-rje-mdzes-'od: 28a.1; Mon-rtse-pa: 12b.7; gTsang-smyon He-ru-ka: 10a.6; dBang-phyug-rgyal-mtshan: 9a.4; lHa-btsun: 6b.4.
10. The *sha-ba*, or *sha-pa*, is the *a-ga-ru* or *a-ka-ru* tree (*Bod-rgya* s.v. *sha-pa*), that is the Aloes-wood, or *Aquilaria agallodum* (M-W s.v. *agaru*).
11. Cf. rGyal-thang-pa: 6a.1; O-rgyan-pa: 7b.6; rDo-rje-mdzes-'od: 28a.3; Mon-rtse-pa: 13a.4; gTsang-smyon He-ru-ka: 10b.2; dBang-phyug-rgyal-mtshan: 10a.7; lHa-btsun: 7a.4.
12. Uḍḍiyāṇa (or *Uḍḍiyāna, Oḍḍiyāṇa, Udyāna, Oḍyāna*; Tib. *U-rgyan* or *O-rgyan*), the birth-place of Padmasambhava, is celebrated as the land of *ḍākinīs*. It is the region of North-West India between Kashmir and the Swat valley (Tucci 1940: 368 ff.).
13. Vajravārāhī (*rDo-rje-phag-mo*), called Jñānaḍākinī (*Ye-shes-mkha'-'gro-ma*) in the following pages, or Bhagavatī Yoginī (*bCom-ldan-rnal-'byor-ma*) and Vajrayoginī (*rDo-rje-rnal-'byor-ma*) in other hagiographies, is the consort of Cakrasaṃvara (De Mallmann 1988: 187-189).

14. Cf. rGyal-thang-pa: 6a.3; O-rgyan-pa: 8a.2; rDo-rje-mdzes-'od: 28a.5; Mon-rtse-pa: 13b.2; gTsang-smyon He-ru-ka: 10b.5; dBang-phyug-rgyal-mtshan: 10b.2; lHa-btsun: 7b.1.
15. The text has here *Sa-la bhe-ra-ha* but, in the following line [4a.4], we read *bhe-ha-ra* (Skt. *vihāra*).
16. Cāryapa, for which *Tsārya-pa* or *Tsarya(-pa)* is the Tibetan transliteration and *sPyod-pa* the translation, is the abbreviation of Kṛṣṇācārya (*Nag-po-spyod-pa*): the honorific title *ācārya* forms a compound with Kṛṣṇa (*Nag-po*), in turn a Sanskrit version of the Apabhraṃśa Kāṇha or the Prakrit Kānupā (Kāṇhupāda) (Shahidullah 1928: 25; Tagare 1948: 20). Apparently this is not the disciple of Jālandhari (Hāḍipā) and author of the *Dohākoṣa*, but a spiritual descendant of his who bore the same name and is also referred to as Kṛṣṇācārya "the Young" (*rGya-gar chos-'byung*, p. 268; *bKa'-babs bdun-ldan*, p. 44; *Life of Kṛṣṇācārya/Kāṇha*, pp. 83, 87) and who may well be identified as the *ācārya* known as Balin, who was active in the first half of the 11th century (*Deb-ther sngon-po*, pp. 243, 372).
17. Lavapa, alias Kambala (Dowman, 1985: 184), is associated by Tāranātha (*rGya-gar-chos-'byung*: 246; *bKa'-babs bdun-ldan*, chap. iv) with Lalitavajra and with Indrabhūti, while 'Gos Lo-tsā-ba gZhon-nu-dpal (*Deb-ther sngon-po*: 362-363) suggests the possibility of identifying him with Indrabhūti, probably a Indrabhūti II (Snellgrove 1959: I, 12-13).
18. From a merely historical point of view, the Nāgārjuna associated with Tilopa should not be confused with the founder of the Madhyamaka school. In fact, he could be the alchemist of the late 10th century mentioned by al-Bīrūnī (Tucci 1930: 213; Naudou 1968: 85-86). As we read in rGyal-thang-pa (fol. 12b.4) this alchemist can be identified with Advayavajra (*gNyis-med-rdo-rje*), and thus probably with Dāmodara and Maitrīgupta (Tucci 1930: 210, 214). The fact that he was from Karahāṅaka, in South India, as testified by rGyal-thang-pa, is confirmed in the Sanskrit biography of Nāgārjuna edited by Tucci (1930: 215, 219).

19. During the empowerment or consecration the disciple, by means of a subtle purification (Skt. *abhiṣeka* < *abhi-sic* "purify with aspersion of water") is authorized, that is the power (*dbang*) to proceed deeper into the spiritual path is bestowed (*skur*) upon him. Such a path is ritually marked by entering the *maṇḍala* (*maṇḍalapraveśa*). In Vajrayāna literature we usually classify the *tantras* (*rgyud*) into four, viz. *kriyā-*, *caryā-*, *yoga-* and *anuttarayoga-tantra*. Graded in view of four human types, who are at different levels, both intellectual and emotional, each tantric path leads to spiritual realization in a more radical and quicker way than the one below it. In the *anuttarayoga-tantra* (*rnal-'byor-bla-med-kyi rgyud*), the starting point of the path is marked by the first of four empowerments, called the Consecration of the Jar (Skt. *kalaśābhiṣeka*, Tib. *bum-dbang*), which comprises some consecrations—generally six—performed in the lower tantras as well. The most essential aspect of the practice, consisting of the progressive dissolution of any residual dualistic attitude, is actualised by the three higher empowerments, viz. the Secret Consecration (Skt. *guhyābhiṣeka*, Tib. *gsang-ba'i dbang*), the Consecration of the Knowledge of the "*Prajñā*" (Skt. *prajñājñānābhiṣeka*, Tib. *shes-rab-ye-shes-kyi dbang*), and finally the Fourth Consecration (Skt. *caturthābhiṣeka*, Tib. *bzhi-ba'i dbang*).
20. That is the *Śrīguhyasamājatantra*.
21. *brGya-stong-pa*, short form for *She-rab-kyi pha-rol-tu-phyin-pa stong-phrag-brgya-pa*, Skt. *Śatasāhasrikā-prajñāpāramitā*. We will be informed later (chap. 2) that Tilopa's uncle was the abbot of the Aśoka-vihāra in East India.
22. We can detect from what follows that the "woman" is the *ḍākinī* Subhaginī (*sKal-ba-bzang-mo*).
23. That is the *Hevajratantra* and the *Cakrasaṃvaratantra*.
24. They are the Developing Stage (Tib. *bskyed-rim*, Skt. *utpatti-krama*) and the Fulfilment Stage (Tib. *rdzogs-rim*, Skt. *sampannakrama*).
25. From the Sanskrit word *tila* "sesame".

26. Even from the lexical point of view we have here a clear allusion to Interdependent Origination, *pratītyasamutpāda*, whose Tibetan translation is *rten-cing-'brel-bar-'byung-ba*, or simply *rten-'brel*.
27. The term *sahaja*, literally meaning "born or produced (Skt. *-ja*, Tib. *skyes-pa*) together or at the same time as (Skt. *saha-*, Tib. *lhan-cig*)", has been translated by Shahidullah (1928) and Snellgrove (1959) as "the Innate". Dasgupta (1946) left it untranslated. Eliade (1954) interpreted it as "le non-conditionné", Bharati (1965) as "the pure and natural state". Lessing and Wayman (1968) went back to a more literal meaning with "together born". So did Guenther (1969) with "coemergence", and Kvaerne (1977) with "co-emergent" and "simultaneously-arisen". Kvaerne (1977: 62) justifies the latter translation because the term "is basically connected with the tantric ritual of consecration, where it refers to the relation between the ultimate and the preliminary stages of Bliss." In fact, "the Fourth, the Ultimate Bliss in which all duality is abolished—arises simultaneously with the Third Bliss."
28. Cfr. rDo-rje-mdzes-'od: 35a.6. Western readers can find two alternative versions of this song in Gyaltsen and Rogers (1986: 58), and in the *Great Kagyu Masters* (p. 45).
29. The reference here is to one of the eight antidotes to prevent the five faults to mental quiescence meditation (Tib. *zhi-gnas*, Skt. *śamatha*).
30. The name of Subhaginī (*sKal-ba-bzang-mo*) is attested in O-rgyan-pa, rDo-rje-mdzes-'od, Mon-rtse-pa and Kun-dga'-rin-chen, while, in gTsang-smyon He-ru-ka, lHa-btsun and dbang-phyug-rgyal-mtshan, we find Samantabhadrī Yoginī (*Kun-tu-bzang-mo'i rNal-'byor-ma*), or Sumatī Samantabhadrī Yoginī. In the bsTan-'gyur (*rGyud-'grel*) there is a work by Tilopa himself in which we can find information about his "human" gurus: *Ṣaḍdharmopadeśa* (*Chos drug-gi man-ngag*), vol. *pu* fol. 129b.2 of the sNar-thang edition, vol. *pu* fol. 134b.2 of the Peking (Cordier, vol. LXXIII, no. 27; *TT*, vol. LXXIII, no. 4630, pp. 34-5), vol. *zhi* fol. 270a.7 of the sDe-dge (*Tôhoku*, no.

2330), vol. *zhi* fol. 270a.6 of the Ço-ne -271a.2. This text, concerning the so-called Six Yogas of Nāropa, assigns them to four gurus: Cāryapa, Nāgārjuna, Lavapa and Sukhasiddhi. Mention is made of the "*ḍākinī*" Sukhasiddhī contemporary with Nāropa's consort Niguma in the *Deb-ther sngon-po* (p. 731), where she is associated with a Virūpa, evidently the Virūpa active in the 11th century (Dowman 1985: 52). Moreover, there are good reasons for identifying both, Subhaginī and Samantabhadrī Yoginī, with the Sukhasiddhī attested in the *Ṣaḍdharmopadeśa.*

31. Cf. O-rgyan-pa: 11b.2; rDo-rje-mdzes-'od: 35a.4; Mon-rtse-pa: 16b.5; gTsang-smyon He-ru-ka: 13b.5; dBang-phyug-rgyal-mtshan: 16b.2; lHa-btsun: 11b.3.
32. Scholars are inevitably faced with the problem of these "transmissions", which is concisely summed up in the English "Introduction" to Mon-rte-pa (pp. 2-3): "Tradition records that Tilopa received four distinct currents (*bka'-babs*) which he passed on to Nāropa; unfortunately Tibetan sources differ considerably as to the lineage and content of each of these currents". The *Ṣaḍdharmopadeśa* assigns instruction to the four *gurus* thus—Cāryapa: *caṇḍālī;* Nāgārjuna: *māyākāya* and *prabhāsvara;* Lavapa: *svapna;* Sukhasiddhī: intermediate state (Tib. *bar-do,* Skt. *antarābhava*) and transference (Tib. *'pho-ba,* Skt. *saṃkrānti*). In Mar-pa—Cāryapa: *svapna.* Nāgārjuna, Mātaṅgīpa: *Guhyasamāja* and *māyākāya.* Lavapa: *prabhāsvara.* Subhaginī: *Hevajra, Cakrasaṃvara,* and *caṇḍālī.* rGyal-thang-pa (fols. 9b.7-13b) gives a different account of the four lineages—Vajrapāṇi, Saraha, Lūipa, Dārikapa, Ḍeṅgipa: *Catuḥpiṭha* and *saṃkrānti.* Sumati Samantabhadrī, Thang-lo-pa, Shing-lo-pa, Karṇaripa: *Mahāmāya, svapna* and *māyākāya.* Ratnamati, Nāgārjuna (alias Advayavajra), Mātaṅgīpa: *Cakrasaṃvara, mahāmudrā* and *yuganaddha.* Vajrapāṇi, Ḍombi Heruka, Lavapa: *Hevajra, prabhāsvara* and *caṇḍālī.*

    If O-rgyan-pa (fol. 11b-1) goes no further than mentioning Cāryapa, Nāgārjuna, Lavapa and Subhaginī without associating them with any teaching, rDo-rje-mdzes-'od (fols. 33b.1-35a) indicates six lines of transmission: two non-human, four human. The first two are oral instruction beyond words (*snyan-rgyud yi-ge-med-pa*) received directly from the *ḍākinī* Vajrayoginī in Uḍḍiyāṇa and the various tantric cycles received from the *bodhisattva* Vajrapāṇi. The four human masters are indicated with relevant teachings—Cāryapa: *Cakrasaṃvara, hetu-mārga-phala* and *caṇḍālī*. Nāgārjuna: *Guhyasamāja, māyākāya* and *prabhāsvara*. Lavapa, Lalitavajra (*Rol-pa-rdo-rje*): *Hevajra, antarābhava* and *prabhāsvara*. Subhaginī: *Śrī-Ḍākārṇava-mahātantrarāja, karmamudrā, saṃkranti* and *antarābhava*. Lūipa, Vijayapāda (*rNam-par-rgyal-ba*): *Cakrasaṃvara*. Saraha, Śavareśvara (*Ri-khrod-dbang-phyug*): *mahāmudrā*.

If Mon-rtse-pa (fol. 16b.3) sets out the information contained in Mar-pa once again, the apparent intention of gTsang-smyon He-ru-ka (fol. 13b.3), and of lHa-btsun (fol. 11b.1) who closely complies with his *guru*, was to complete and integrate the *Ṣaḍdharmopadeśa* and Mar-pa—Cāryapa: *caṇḍālī* and *svapna*. Nāgārjuna: *māyākāya*. Lavapa: *prabhāsvara*. Sumati Samatabhadrī: *saṃkrānti* and *antarābhava*. The other disciple of gTsang-smyon, dBang-phyug-rgyal-mtshan (fols. 16a.1-16b), seems to reconcile the evident discrepancies we find in the other *rnam-thars*, at least in terms of lineages. In fact, he distinguishes between two lines of transmission: an ordinary (*thun-mongs*) and an extra-ordinary (*thun-mongs-ma-yin-pa*) one. (1) *Thun-mongs-kyi bka'-babs*—Vajrapāṇi, Saraha, Lūipa, Dārikapa, Ḍeṅgipa: *mahāmudrā*. Ratnamati, Nāgārjuna, Mātaṅgīpa: *pitṛ-tantra*. Sumati Samantabhadrī, Shing-lo-pa, Thang-lo-pa, Karṇaripa: *mātṛ-tantra*. Virūpa (*Bhir-wa-pa*), Ḍombi Heruka, Bhi-na-sa, Lavapa, Indrabhūti: *advaita-tantra* and *prabhāsvara*. (2) *Thun-mongs-ma-yin-pa'i bka'-babs*—Cāryapa: *caṇḍālī* and *svapna*. Nāgārjuna: *māyākāya* and *pitṛ-tantra*. Lavapa: *prabhās-vara* and *advaita-tantra*. Sumati Samantabhadrī: *saṃkrānti, antarābhava* and *mātṛ-tantra*.

33. Cf. O-rgyan-pa: 8a.3; rDo-rje-mdzes-'od: 28b.1; dBang-phyug-rgyal-mtshan: 10b.3.
34. Cf. O-rgyan-pa: 8a.3; rDo-rje-mdzes-'od: 28b.2; dBang-phyug-rgyal-mtshan: 10b.4; lHa-btsun: 10a.1.
35. For this uncommon word, other texts have *byi-gzungs*, *bye-gzungs*, or *byi-zun-thun*.
36. Cf. rGyal-thang-pa: 6b.5; O-rgyan-pa: 9a.1; rDo-rje-mdzes-'od: 29a.2; Mon-rtse-pa: 14a.5; gTsang-smyon He-ru-ka: 11a.5; dBang-phyug-rgyal-mtshan: 11a.5; lHa-btsun: 8a.3.
37. Cf. O-rgyan-pa: 9a.1; rDo-rje-mdzes-'od: 29a.3; gTsang-smyon He-ru-ka: 11a.6; dBang-phyug-rgyal-mtshan: 11a.7; lHa-btsun: 8a.3.
38. Cf. rGyal-thang-pa: 6b.7; O-rgyan-pa: 9a.3; rDo-rje-mdzes-'od: 29a.5; gTsang-smyon He-ru-ka: 11a.7; dBang-phyug-rgyal-mtshan: 11b.1; lHa-btsun: 8a.5.
39. Cf. O-rgyan-pa: 9a.3; rDo-rje-mdzes-'od: 29a.6; Mon-rtse-pa: 14b.1; gTsang-smyon He-ru-ka: 11a.7; dBang-phyug-rgyal-mtshan: 11b.2; lHa-btsun: 8a.6.
40. Cf. rGyal-thang-pa: 7a.1; O-rgyan-pa: 9a.4; rDo-rje-mdzes-'od: 29b.2; Mon-rtse-pa: 14b.4; gTsang-smyon He-ru-ka: 11b.2; dBang-phyug-rgyal-mtshan: 11b.3; lHa-btsun: 8b.2.
41. Cf. rDo-rje-mdzes-'od: 29b.3; dBang-phyug-rgyal-mtshan: 11b.4; lHa-btsun: 8b.2.
42. Cf. O-rgyan-pa: 9b.2; rDo-rje-mdzes-'od: 29b.4; dBang-phyug-rgyal-mtshan: 11b.6; lHa-btsun: 8b.4.
43. Cf. rGyal-thang-pa: 7b.2; O-rgyan-pa: 9b.4; rDo-rje-mdzes-'od: 30a.1; Mon-rtse-pa: 15a.3; gTsang-smyon He-ru-ka: 11b.6; dBang-phyug-rgyal-mtshan: 12a.4; lHa-btsun: 9a.1.
44. Cf. rGyal-thang-pa: 7b.4; O-rgyan-pa: 9b.4; rDo-rje-mdzes-'od: 30a.2; Mon-rtse-pa: 15a.4; gTsang-smyon He-ru-ka: 11b.7; dBang-phyug-rgyal-mtshan: 12a.6; lHa-btsun: 9a.2.
45. In gTsang-smyon He-ru-ka and lHa-btsun-pa also the meditative evocation (Skt. *bhāvanā*, Tib. *sgom-pa*) is mentioned: *blta bsgom spyod-pa 'bras-bu'ang*. Of these three—*dṛṣṭi*, *bhāvanā*, and *caryā*—Guenther (1958: 80-81) remarks: "[The] intuitive character of Eastern systems of philosophy is

evident from the very words used for what we designate by philosophy, viz. "seeing, view" (*lta-ba*, Skt. *dṛṣṭi, darśana*). Philosophy which thus is the Seeing of Reality is not the culmination of one's abilities but the very beginning of the arduous task of achieving spiritual maturity. In this way philosophy in the Eastern sense of the word only serves to clear the way and, quite literally, to open the student's eyes. What he sees has to be closely attended to (*sgom-pa*, Skt. *bhāvanā*) and must be actually lived (*spyod-pa*, Skt. *caryā*)." In another article Guenther (1966-67: 179) stresses that view, evocative meditation, and action are "facets, not parts, of human being. Neither can they be added up nor separated."

46. Cf. O-rgyan-pa: 9b.6; rDo-rje-mdzes-'od: 30a.4; gTsang-smyon He-ru-ka: 12a.3; dBang-phyug-rgyal-mtshan: 12b.2; lHa-btsun: 9a.5.
47. Cf. O-rgyan-pa: 10b.1; rDo-rje-mdzes-'od: 31b.1; Mon-rtse-pa:15b.6; gTsang-smyon He-ru-ka: 12b.4; dBang-phyug-rgyal-mtshan: 13a.6; lHa-btsun: 10a.2.
48. Cf. O-rgyan-pa: 10b.2; rDo-rje-mdzes-'od: 31b.3; Mon-rtse-pa: 16a.2; gTsang-smyon He-ru-ka: 12b.5, 13a.1; lHa-btsun: 10b.2.
49. In gTsang-smyon He-ru-ka (fol. 12a.4), dBang-phyug-rgyal-mtshan (fol. 12b.4) and lHa-btsuṅ-pa (fol. 9a.6) the three signs are characterized thus: *sku bde-mchog lhan-skyes yab-yum-gyi rtsa-ka-li gcig dang / gsung rdo-rje chos-byung-la bai-du-rya'i yi-ge bdun-(ba) bris-pa gcig dang / thugs bai-du-rya'i rdo-rje rtse-lnga-pa gcig rnams bstan.*
50. The first term of this *dvandva* refers to "a complex phenomenon of mental activity and in the widest sense of the word it expresses the ordinary dual mode of cognition involving a perceiving subject which owns the specific perceptual situation (*yul-can*) and the perceptual situation with its sense-field and sensum therein (*yul*)." (Guenther 1956: 43). Cfr. *Tillopādasya Dohākoṣa, dohā* 32 of the Bagchi edition (1938): *vaṇṇa vi vajjaï ākī-vihuṇṇā / savvāāre so saṃpuṇṇā*, with its Tibetan version (*Do-ha mdzod*) in the *bsTan-'gyur* (*rGyud-'grel*), vol. *tsi* fol. 135b.5 of the sNar-thang edition, vol. *tsi*

fol. 147b.1 of the Peking (Cordier, vol. XLVII, no. 22; *TT*, vol. LXIX, no. 3128, p. 131), vol. *zhi* fol. 136a.4 of the sDe-dge (*Tôhoku*, no. 2281), vol. *zhi* fol. 136a.6 of the Co-ne: *kha dog spangs shing rig med pa // snang ba thams cad de la rdzogs*, where Tib. *snang-ba* is for *āāra* (Skt. *ākāra*).

51. Cf. rGyal-thang-pa: 8a.4; O-rgyan-pa: 10a.2; rDo-rje-mdzes-'od: 30b.6; Mon-rtse-pa: 15b.2; gTsang-smyon He-ru-ka: 12a.6; dBang-phyug-rgyal-mtshan: 12b.6; lHa-btsun: 9b.2.
52. As H. Guenther (1952: 61 n. 1) observes, "*prajñā* is a *caitta* or mental event belonging to the group of five called *niyata-viṣaya* "object-determined", and is defined as *dharmāṇām pravicaya* "analysis of entities" emphasizing its selective and appreciative character. *Prajñā* is a function which developed to its highest point (*pāramitā*) becomes a "transcending function". The translation of this term by "wisdom" is hardly justified..."
53. Cf. rGyal-thang-pa: 8a.5; O-rgyan-pa: 10a.3; rDo-rje-mdzes-'od: 31a.2; Mon-rtse-pa: 15b.3; gTsang-smyon He-ru-ka: 12a.7; dBang-phyug-rgyal-mtshan: 13a.1; lHa-btsun: 9b.4.
54. Cf. *Tillopādasya Dohākoṣa, dohā 33*: "This mental activity is to be promptly killed; no supports to the thinking activity: such is the *mahāmudrā*, stainless in three worlds!" (*e maṇa mārahu lahu citte ṇimmūla / tahi mahāmudda tihuaṇe ṇimmala*, Skt.: *etat manaḥ māraya śīghraṃ citte nirmūlam / tasmāt mahāmudrā tribhuvane nirmalā [bhavati]*). The Tibetan version is different: *yid ni sod la sems ni rtsa ba med par gyis // sems kyi lhag ma zug rngu thong // 'di ru sku bzhi phyag rgya bzhi // khams gsum ma lus de tshe dag*. Anyway, the allusion to the four *mudrās* connected with the four *kāyas* is confirmed by the Sanskrit commentary (*pañjikā*) of this *dohā*.
55. Cf. rGyal-thang-pa: 8a.7; O-rgyan-pa: 10b.2; rDo-rje-mdzes-'od: 31b.5; Mon-rtse-pa: 15b.7; gTsang-smyon He-ru-ka: 12b.2, 12b.6; dBang-phyug-rgyal-mtshan: 13b.1; lHa-btsun: 10a.5.

56. Cf. rGyal-thang-pa: 8b.3; O-rgyan-pa: 10b.5; rDo-rje-mdzes-'od: 32a.4; Mon-rtse-pa: 16a.3; gTsang-smyon He-ru-ka: 13a.2; dBang-phyug-rgyal-mtshan: 13b.6; lHa-btsun: 10b.3.
57. So it is specified in O-rgyan-pa (fol. 11a.1): *de-nas bde'-mchog rtsa-rgyud le'u lnga-bcu-pa-cig.*
58. Cf. rGyal-thang-pa: 8b.5; O-rgyan-pa: 11a.1; rDo-rje-mdzes-'od: 32b.4; Mon-rtse-pa: 16a.4; gTsang-smyon He-ru-ka: 13a.4; Kun-dga'-rin-chen: 13b.5; dBang-phyug-rgyal-mtshan: 14a.2.
59. Cf. rGyal-thang-pa: 8b.6; O-rgyan-pa: 11a.2; rDo-rje-mdzes-'od: 32b.5; Mon-rtse-pa: 16a.5; gTsang-smyon He-ru-ka: 13a.5; dBang-phyug-rgyal-mtshan: 14a.4; lHa-btsun: 11a.1.
60. Cf. rGyal-thang-pa: 9a.1; O-rgyan-pa: 11a.3; rDo-rje-mdzes-'od: 33a.1; Mon-rtse-pa: 16a.6; gTsang-smyon He-ru-ka: 13a.6; dBang-phyug-rgyal-mtshan: 14a.4; lHa-btsun: 11a.1.
61. Tilopa transmitted the instructions alluded to in these verses to Nāropa, who passed them to Mar-pa and to the Indian Tiphupa. According to gTsang-smyon He-ru-ka (*Mi-la-ras-pa'i mgur-'bum*: 397-401), Mar-pa passed only four of them to Mi-la-ras-pa, and prophesied that he, or someone else, would go to India to receive the other five. As Mi-la-ras-pa was completely satisfied with the four he had, he never did go to India. It was his disciple Ras-chung-rdo-rje-grags (1084-1161) who accomplished this task. First, he received them in Nepal from a Bharima, maybe the same Bharima connected with Tilopa; then, in India, from Tiphupa himself.
62. Cf. rGyal-thang-pa: 9a.2; O-rgyan-pa: 11a.4; rDo-rje-mdzes-'od: 33a.2; Mon-rtse-pa: 16a.7; gTsang-smyon He-ru-ka: 13a.7; dBang-phyug-rgyal-mtshan: 14b.5; lHa-btsun: 11a.3.
63. Cf. rGyal-thang-pa: 9a.4; O-rgyan-pa: 11a.5; rDo-rje-mdzes-'od: 33a.5; Mon-rtse-pa: 16b.3; gTsang-smyon He-ru-ka: 13b.2; dBang-phyug-rgyal-mtshan: 15a.1; lHa-btsun: 11a.5.
64. Cf. rGyal-thang-pa: 10a.3; O-rgyan-pa: 11b.2; rDo-rje-mdzes-'od: 33b.3; Mon-rtse-pa: 16b.4; gTsang-smyon He-ru-ka: 13b.4; dBang-phyug-rgyal-mtshan: 16a.1; lHa-btsun: 11b.2.

65. Cf. Tilopa's *Acintyamahāmudrā* (*Phyag-rgya-chen-po bsam-gyis-mi-khyab-pa*) in the *bsTan-'gyur* (*rgyud-'grel*), in which his teachings to these eight, after their conversion, are given (*Tôhoku*, no. 2305: *Phyag-rgya chen-po bsam-gyis-mi-khyab-pa zhes-bya-ba*; no. 2306: *mThu-can-la gdams-pa*; no. 2307: *Glu-mkhan-la gdams-pa*; no. 2308: *Mu-stegs-la gdams-pa*; no. 2309: *Shan-pa-la gdams-pa*; no. 2310: *Rig-byed-mkhan-la gdams-pa*; no. 2311: *sGyu-ma-mkhan-la gdams-pa*; no. 2312: *sMad-'tshong-la gdams-pa*).
66. Cf. rGyal-thang-pa: 13b.5; O-rgyan-pa: 11b.3; rDo-rje-mdzes-'od: 35b.6; Mon-rtse-pa: 17a.1; gTsang-smyon He-ru-ka: 14a.1; Kun-dga'-rin-chen: 13a.1; dBang-phyug-rgyal-mtshan: 21a.1; lHa-btsun: 12a.1.
67. The term *ku-sa-li* (Skt. *kuśalī*), or its corrupt form *ku-su-lu* (cf. O-rgyan-pa: 11b.5), refers to those sages, either Hindus or Buddhists, who are more devout than learned.
68. Cf. rGyal-thang-pa: 14b.6; O-rgyan-pa: 12b.2; rDo-rje-mdzes-'od: 37a.2; Mon-rtse-pa: 17b.7; gTsang-smyon He-ru-ka: 14b.6; dBang-phyug-rgyal-mtshan: 22a.7; lHa-btsun: 15a.2.
69. We have here an allusion to the *prāṇayāma* vase-breathing technique (Tib. *bum-pa-can*, Skt. *kumbhaka*).
70. Cf. rGyal-thang-pa: 15a.7; O-rgyan-pa: 13a.4; rDo-rje-mdzes-'od: 38a.4; Mon-rtse-pa: 18a.7; gTsang-smyon He-ru-ka: 15a.7; dBang-phyug-rgyal-mtshan: 23a.7; lHa-btsun: 17a.5.
71. Cf. rGyal-thang-pa: 16a.5; O-rgyan-pa: 14a.4; rDo-rje-mdzes-'od: 37b.3; Mon-rtse-pa: 19a.5; gTsang-smyon He-ru-ka: 15b.7; dBang-phyug-rgyal-mtshan: 24b.1; lHa-btsun: 20a.4.
72. Cf. rGyal-thang-pa: 18b.3; O-rgyan-pa: 17a.3; rDo-rje-mdzes-'od: 40b.1; Mon-rtse-pa: 21a.4; gTsang-smyon He-ru-ka: 17a.7; dBang-phyug-rgyal-mtshan: 28a.1; lHa-btsun: 26b.6.
73. Cf. rGyal-thang-pa: 18a.5; O-rgyan-pa: 16b.2; rDo-rje-mdzes-'od: 40a.2; Mon-rtse-pa: 20b.5; gTsang-smyon He-ru-ka: 17a.2; dBang-phyug-rgyal-mtshan: 27a.6; lHa-btsun: 24b.6.
74. This verse alludes to the *yoga* technique of transference (Tib. *'pho-ba*, Skt. *saṃkrānti*).

75. Cf. rGyal-thang-pa: 17a.3; O-rgyan-pa: 35b.3; rDo-rje-mdzes-'od: 38b.6; Mon-rtse-pa: 20a.1; gTsang-smyon He-ru-ka: 16a.6; dBang-phyug-rgyal-mtshan: 25b.7; lHa-btsun: 22a.5.
76. A follower of Cārvāka, the Indian philosopher whose theories are systematized in the *Bārhaspatyasūtra.* The Lokāyatikas, far from being mere hedonists, would deny (Skt. *nāstika* from *na-asti* "there is not") any empirical basis to the law of *karman*.
77. Cf. rGyal-thang-pa: 19a.1; O-rgyan-pa: 17b.3; rDo-rje-mdzes-'od: 40b.6; Mon-rtse-pa: 21b.1; gTsang-smyon He-ru-ka: 17b.4; dBang-phyug-rgyal-mtshan: 29b.7; lHa-btsun: 29a.1.
78. Cf. rGyal-thang-pa: 19b.3; O-rgyan-pa: 18a.5; rDo-rje-mdzes-'od: 42a.2; Mon-rtse-pa: 22a.1; gTsang-smyon He-ru-ka: 18a.3; dBang-phyug-rgyal-mtshan: 32b.3; lHa-btsun: 31a.5.
79. The "three wheels" (*'khor-lo rnam-gsum*) through which a monk practises *dharma*, viz. (1) the wheel of study through reading, listening and thinking (*klog-pa-thos-bsam-gyi 'khor-lo*), (2) the wheel of abandonment through concentration (*spong-ba-bsam-gtan-gyi 'khor-lo*), and (3) the wheel of service through activities (*bya-ba-las-kyi 'khor-lo*).
80. The ten spiritual trainings of a monk (*chos-spyod bcu*) are (1) writing (*yi-ge 'bri-ba*), (2) worshipping (*mchod-pa 'bul-ba*), (3) developing generosity (*sbyin-pa gtong-ba*), (4) hearing the *dharma* (*chos nyan-pa*), (5) memorizing (*'dzin-pa*), (6) reading (*klog-pa*), (7) explaining (*'chad-pa*), (8) reciting (*kha-ton-du bya-ba*), (9) thinking over the *dharma* (*chos-kyi don sems-pa*), and (10) attending meditatively to it (*chos-kyi don sgom-pa*).
81. Cf. rGyal-thang-pa: 20a.5; O-rgyan-pa: 25a.3; rDo-rje-mdzes-'od: 42a.6; Mon-rtse-pa: 22b.5; gTsang-smyon He-ru-ka: 18b.7; dBang-phyug-rgyal-mtshan: 35b.6; lHa-btsun: 32a.6.
82. Logic (*gnas-tshigs-rig-pa*) is one of the five fields of study (*rig-gnas che-ba lnga*), the others being arts and crafts (*bzo-rig-pa*), medicine (*gso-ba-rig-pa*), grammar (*sgra-rig-pa*), and philosophy (*nang-don-rig-pa*).

83. Cf. rGyal-thang-pa: 20b.4; O-rgyan-pa: 25a.5; rDo-rje-mdzes-'od: 42b.4; Mon-rtse-pa: 23a.6; gTsang-smyon He-ru-ka: 19b.1; dBang-phyug-rgyal-mtshan: 37b.2; lHa-btsun: 33a.2.

References

dBang-phyug-rgyal-mtshan:

Ms. A—*Bka' brgyud gser 'phreṅ rgyas pa. A reproduction of an incomplete manuscript of a collection of the lives of the successive masters of the 'Brug-pa Dkar-brgyud-pa tradition reflecting the tradition of Rdzoṅ-khul in Zaṅs-dkar established by Grub-dbaṅ Ṅag-dbaṅ-tshe-riṅ, reproduced from a manuscript preserved in Zaṅs-dkar.* (Kargyud Sungrab Nyamso Khang) Darjeeling, 1982, vol. I, pp. 9-97.

Ms. B—*The biographies of Tilopa and Naropa by Dbaṅ-phyug-rgyal-mtshan. Rje btsun Ti lo pa'i rnam par thar pa zab gsal rin chen gter mdzod bskal bzaṅ yid 'phrog. Mkhas mchog Nā ro Paṇ chen gyi rnam par thar pa dri med legs bśad bde chen 'brug sgra. Reproduced from a manuscript from Dzongkhul Monastery in Zangskar.* (Kargyud Sungrab Nyamso Khang) Darjeeling, 1976, pp. 1-157.

Bharati, A. (1965) *The Tantric Tradition*, London.

Bod-rgya tshig-mdzod chen-mo (1986) Beijing.

Chang, G.C.C. (1962) *Mi-la-ras-pa'i mgur-'bum/ The Hundred Thousand Songs of Milarepa*, Boulder-London (1977).

Chatterji, S.K. (1926) *Origin and Development of the Bengali Language*, Calcutta.

Chattopadhyaya, A. (1967) *Atīśa and Tibet. Life and Works of Dīpaṃkara Śrījñāna in relation to the History and Religion of Tibet. With Tibetan Sources translated under Professor Lama Chimpa*, Calcutta.

Cordier, P. (1909-1915) *Catalogue du fonds tibétain*, Paris.

Dasgupta, S. (1946) *Obscure Religious Cults*, Calcutta.

De, S.K. (1943) in R.C. Majumdar (ed.), *History of Bengal*, Dacca.

De Mallmann, M.Th. (1986) *Introduction à l'iconographie du Tântrisme bouddhique*, Paris.

rDo-rje-mdzes-'od *Bka' brgyud kyi rnam thar chen mo rin po che'i gter mdzod dgos 'dod 'byuṅ gnas. A collection of lives of the successive masters in the transmission lineage of the 'Bri-guṅ Bka'-brgyud-pa tradition in the Nepal-Tibet borderlands by Rdo-rje-mdzes-'od, reproduced from a rare manuscript from Limi Dzing Pegyeling*, n.p., 1985, pp. 53-86.

Dowman, K. (1985) *Masters of Mahāmudrā. Songs and Histories of the Eighty-Four Buddhist Siddhas*, New York.

Eliade, M. (1954) *Le Yoga. Immortalité et liberté*, Paris.

sGam-po-pa *Collected works (gsuṅ 'bum) of Sgam-po-pa Bsod-nams-rin-chen. Reproduced from a manuscript from Bkra-śis-chos-rdzoṅ Monastery in Miyad Lahul by Khasdub Gyatsho Shashin*, Delhi, 1975, pp. 1-16.

Guenther, H.V. (1952) *Yuganaddha. The Tantric View of Life*, Varanasi.

______ (1956) "The Concept of Mind in Buddhist Tantrism", *Journal of Oriental Studies*, III, Hong Kong (then in *TBWP*).

______ (1958) "The Levels of Understanding in Buddhism", *Journal of the American Oriental Society*, vol. 78, New Haven (then in *TBWP*).

______ (1959-60) "The Philosophical Background of Buddhist Tantrism", *Journal of Oriental Society*, vol. V, Hong Kong (then in *TBWP*).

______ (1963/1) "Indian Buddhist Thought in Tibetan Perspective—Infinite Transcendence versus Finiteness", in *History of Religions*, vol. III, no. 1, Chicago (then in *TBWP*).

_____ (1963/2) *The Life and Teachings of Nāropa*, London.

_____ (1966) "Mentalism and Beyond in Buddhist Philosophy", *Journal of the American Oriental Society*, vol. 86, New Haven (then in *TBWP*).

_____ (1966-67) "Le maître spirituel en Tibet", *Hermes*, Paris (then in *TBWP*).

_____ (1968) "Tantra and Revelation", in *History of Religions*, vol. VII, no. 4, Chicago (then in *TBWP*).

_____ (1969) *The Royal Song of Saraha. A Study in the History of Buddhist Thought*, Seattle.

_____ (1977) *Tibetan Buddhism in Western Perspective* (TBWP). *Collected Articles of Herbert V. Guenther*, Emeryville.

rGyal-thang-pa *Dkar brgyud gser 'phreṅ. A thirteenth century collection of verse hagiographies of the succession of eminent masters of the 'Brug-pa Dkar-brgyud-pa tradition by Rgyal-thaṅ-pa Bde-chen-rdo-rje, reproduced from a rare manuscript from the library of the Hemis Monastery by the 8th Khams-sprul Don-brgyud-ñi-ma*, (Sungrab Nyamso Gyunphel Parkhang) Tashijong Palampur, 1973, pp. 16-57.

Gyaltsen, K.K. & K.L. Rogers (1986) *The Garland of Mahamudra Practices*, New York.

Gyaltsen, K.K. & V. Huckenpahler (1990) *The Great Kagyu Masters. The Golden Lineage Treasury*, New York.

lHa-btsun:

Ms. A—*Rare Dkar-brgyud-pa texts from Himachal Pradesh. A collection of biographical works and philosophical treatises, reproduced from prints from ancient western Tibetan blocks by Urgyan Dorje*, New Delhi, 1976, pp. 37-83.

Ms. B—*Bka'-brgyud-pa Hagiographies. A collection of rnam-thar of eminent masters of Tibetan Buddhism.*

Compiled and edited by Khams-sprul Don-brgyud-ñi-ma, (Sungrab Nyamso Gyunphel Parkhang) Tashijong Palampur, 1972, vol. I, pp. 1-75.

Kun-dga'-rin-chen *Miscellaneous writings (bka' 'bum thor bu) of 'Bri-gung Chos-rje Kun-dga'-rin-chen. Reproduced from the rare manuscripts from the library of Tokden Rinpoche of Gangon, containing a biography of Chos-rgyal Phun-tshogs-bkra-shis (1547-1602),* (Smanrtsis Shesrig Spendzod, vol. 27) Leh, 1972, pp. 22-26.

Kvaerne, P. (1977) *An Anthology of Buddhist Tantric Songs,* Oslo.

Lama Chimpa & A. Chattopadhyaya (1970) *rGya-gar chos-'byung Tāranātha's History of Buddhism in India,* Simla (Calcutta 1980).

Lessing, F.D. & A. Wayman (1968) *Introduction to the Buddhist Tantric Systems,* The Hague.

Mar-pa *Bde mchog mkha' 'gro sñan rgyud (Ras chuṅ sñan rgyud). A manuscript collection of orally transmitted precepts focussing upon the tutelaries Cakrasamvara and Vajravārāhī, representing the yig-cha compiled by Byaṅ-chub-bzaṅ-po, reproduced from a rare manuscript in the library of Apho Rimpoche,* New Delhi, 1973, vol. I, pp. 8-28.

Mon-rtse-pa *Dkar brgyud gser 'phreng. A golden rosary of lives of eminent gurus. Compiled by Mon-rtse-pa Kun-dga'-dpal-ldan and edited by Kun-dga'-'brug-dpal. Reproduced photographically from the original Bhotia manuscript with an English introduction,* (Smanrtsis Shesrig Spendzod, vol. 3) Leh, 1970.

Monier-Williams, M. (1899) *A Sanskrit-English Dictionary,* Oxford.

Naudou, J. (1968) *Les Bouddhistes Kaśmīriens au Moyen Âge,* Paris.

O-rgyan-pa *Bka' brgyud yid bźin nor bu yi 'phreṅ ba. A precious rosary of lives of eminent masters of the 'Bri-guṅ pa Dkar-brgyud-pa tradition by Grub-thob O-rgyan-pa Rin-chen-dpal. Reproduced from a rare manuscript containing three supplemental biographies of teachers of the Smar-pa Dkar-brgyud-pa tradition from the library of the Ven. Kangyur Rinpoche,* (Smanrtsis Shesrig Spendzod, vol. 38) Leh, 1972, pp. 14-52.

Roerich, G.N. (1949) *Deb-ther sngon-po, The Blue Annals.* Calcutta (Delhi 1979).

Shahidullah, M. (1928) *Les chants mystiques de Kāṇha et de Saraha. Les Dohā-koṣa (en apabhraṃśa, avec les versions tibétaines) et les Caryā (en vieux-bengali)*, Paris.

Snellgrove, D.L. (1959) *The Hevajra Tantra*, London.

Tagare, G.V. (1948) *Historical Grammar of Apabhraṃśa*, Poona (Delhi 1987).

Templeman, D. (1983) *Tāranātha's bKa'-babs-bdun-ldan/ The Seven Instruction Lineages by Jo-nang-Tāranātha*, Dharamsala.

______ (1983) *Tāranātha's Life of Kṛṣṇācārya/Kāṇha*, Dharamsala.

Tibetan-English Dictionary of Buddhist Terminology (TEDBT) Nang-don rig-pa'i ming-tshig bod-dbyin shan-sbyar (revised and enlarged edition, 1993), Tsepak Rigzin, Dharamsala.

Tibetan Tripiṭaka, The: Peking Edition, ed D.T. Suzuki, Tokyo-Kyoto.

Tillopadāsya Dohākoṣa Bagchi, P.C. (1938) *Dohākoṣa*, Calcutta.

gTsang-smyon He-ru-ka:

Ms. A—*bDe mchog mkha' 'gro snyan rgyud (Ras chung snyan rgyud). Two manuscript collections of texts from the yig cha of Gtsang-smyon He-ru-ka. Reproduced from 16th and 17th century manuscripts belonging to the Venerable*

Dookpa Thosay Rinpoche, vol. I—*The Biography of Gtsang-smyon by Lha-btsun Rin-chen-rnam-rgyal - The Bya-btang 'Phrin-las-dpal-'bar Manuscript,* (Smanrtsis Shesrig Spendzod, vol. 11) Leh, 1971, pp. 22-43.

Ms. B—*bDe mchog mkha' 'gro snyan rgyud (Ras chung snyan rgyud). Two manuscript collections of texts from the yig cha of Gtsang-smyon He-ru-ka. Reproduced from 16th and 17th century manuscripts belonging to the Venerable Dookpa Thosay Rinpoche,* vol. II—*The Gra-dkar Rab-'jam-pa Manuscript,* (Smanrtsis Shesrig Spendzod, vol. 12) Leh, 1971, pp. 97-118.

Tucci, G. (1930) "Animadversiones Indicae", *Journal of the Asiatic Society of Bengal,* xxvi (then in *Opera minora,* Rome 1971).

______ (1940) *The Travels of Tibetan Pilgrims in the Swat Valley,* Calcutta (then in *Opera minora,* Rome 1971).

______ (1949) *Tibetan Painted Scrolls,* Rome.

Ui, H., M. Suzuki, Y. Kanakura & T. Tada (1934) *Tôhoku/ A Catalogue-Index of the Tibetan Buddhist Canons (Bkaḥ-ḥgyur and Bstan-ḥgyur),* Sendai.